# Bagels
# & Bacon

# Bagels & Bacon

## THE POST-WAR EAST END

Jeff Rozelaar

The History Press

First published 2011
Reprinted 2017, 2018

The History Press
The Mill, Brimscombe Port
Stroud, Gloucestershire, GL5 2QG
www.thehistorypress.co.uk

British Library Cataloguing in Publication Data.
A catalogue record for this book is available from the British Library.

ISBN 978 0 7524 5870 0

Typesetting and origination by The History Press
Printed in Great Britain by TJ International Ltd, Padstow, Cornwall

# Contents

# one

# Starters

I don't remember the first day of my life. I have never forgotten the eighth, though, when I was circumcised. My mother Nancy always treated this claim with disbelief, my future wife Susan with amusement. I retain a vivid picture of male figures, one of whom was my paternal grandfather, clustered around an operating table. They were observing the skills of the *mo'hel* (the semi-medical, quasi-religious individual) who traditionally removes the foreskin from the tiny penises of protesting Jewish boys. A trick of memory? A snap of my snip! Hampton Court was where I made my debut. Not the royal palace but the Bearsted Memorial Hospital, an establishment of lesser majesty a few yards down the road. Witty friends would tweak its name, claiming my parents never married.

This suburban sanctuary was chosen since in 1944 it was raining V1s on E1. The Second World War even had pre-natal influence on my formation and an edgy disposition may well have been implanted in the womb. A pregnant Nancy bravely, but perhaps unwisely, volunteered to conduct London buses through earlier air raids. As her 653s motored along the Mile End Road, dodging falling bombs, my frenzied foetus must have twitched at every explosion. The spiral staircases of her double-deckers and the sudden pings of her ticket machine may have further damaged my nerves.

Legend has it that, early in her career, at one 'request' stop, the sirens sounded an alert. The passengers were divided as to what the next step should be. Abandon the vulnerable vehicle and seek the nearest shelter, or turn a deaf ear and, with luck, arrive home on time. Nancy suggested that they put the options to a speedy show of trembling hands. Her customers agreed to my mother's proposal. She then proceeded to conduct the voting. The result favoured the brave, and fortunately a god of transport sheltered the travellers under a divine hand. The bus completed its scheduled journey without a scratch on its bright

My grandfather George. After the First World War he set himself up in the bookmaking business under the name of 'Captain Webb'.

red paint. On hearing the saga in the canteen depot, Nancy's fellow public servants raised chipped mugs of dark brown tea in professional admiration. In this small way, my mother's telling action had proved that a tiny flame of democracy could burn alongside the larger flames of the Blitz.

My father Henry's war record, however, contained no such heroic tale. I recall a photograph of him in a standard private's uniform with a forage cap tilted at a rakish angle. Beside him, at ease, stood a self-conscious group of grinning squaddies. Blobs of snow blurred the image but, in spite of the absence of greatcoats and gloves, the evident icy temperature appeared not to bother them. Henry's employment within the army was to act as batman (personal servant) to a lieutenant. Henry was mildly amused that the officer's peacetime occupation had been to 'floor walk', in a supervisory capacity, the aisles of a Woolworth's store. How well-shined his shoes were as he passed the counters of cheap goods is not known, but Henry assured me proudly that his military boots never lacked a sparkle.

Ironically it was his feet that ended Henry's service to his king. He had flat ones. These misshapen body parts prevented him being shipped to Singapore in 1942. There he would have been part of the huge garrison that was later to surrender. He candidly admitted that he would not have survived the ordeal of imprisonment by the Emperor of Japan. When I gaze down idly from time to time at my own inherited and identical 'plates of meat', I realise that I owe my very existence to what I stand on daily.

Back in Civvy Street, Henry joined the Rag Trade. My birth certificate registers Henry as a tailor. This cut little dash in the wartime property market and my first 'at homes' were in consequence in my maternal grandmother Rebecca's council flat – No. 5 Herbert House, Goulston Street. This was not the healthiest environment for a newborn babe as its front door stood beside a communal dust chute. Behind its noisy door, a metallic container received the chuckable waste of five storeys of inhabitants. This second, if not malevolent, bombardment further nuked my nascent nerves, as well as fine-tuning my sense of smell.

A photograph found in the effects of a recently deceased uncle fuels speculation about my appearance at that time. My grandmother and her youngest daughter, my Aunt Kitty, are standing above my seated mother. The latter is gazing fondly at something in her lower arms out of shot. One assumes I am the missing item. Why did the photographer leave out the newborn babe? Was this a deliberate comment on my appearance? Was the unknown cameraman distracted at the crucial moment? Or was he simply bad at his job?

Independent living for my parents and me started a few years later. Just a short distance away in Stoney Lane stood the impossibly named Barnett's

Mansions, where Henry had the key to No. 4 at seven shillings and sixpence a week. Whoever conjured up the building's title had a wicked sense of irony, for it was far from a palatial residence. The flats were built above Barnett's, a kosher butcher's shop with a high ceiling, tiled walls and saw-dusted floor. Our kitchen and living room at the rear overlooked the factory part of the premises. From there an aroma of manipulated meat wafted up daily in clouds of oddly scented steam.

Through the vapour three other tenement blocks were visible. These bore a more accurate description. During Benjamin Disraeli's premiership a long-gone parliament had passed an Artisans' and Labourers' Dwellings Act. A mason had inscribed the details on a foundation stone, a history lesson on a grimy wall. Our accommodation was a fraction superior. Those residing in Dizzy's domiciles had to share their kitchen and other conveniences.

In the yards between these building blocks, I later joined other boys in a number of improvised games. On one memorable occasion, we chalked an oval circuit to simulate a speedway track. The idea was inspired by the visits of older lads to Wembley. Their attention had been gripped, not by the roar of a football crowd, but by that of racing engines. This soundtrack was accompanied by a visual spectacular of thrills and spills. My friends and I attempted to simulate the whole event by frantic running and barging, while our inadequate voices vainly tried to convey the noises of the bikes without brakes.

An occupant of the most distant block was Brian Albert. He resided unusually with his mother, uncle and grandmother – the latter a famous victim of the locality's love of nicknames. She was only ever referred to as 'Sarah Sideways'. The unflattering description was used unashamedly (but not to her face) and referred to her inclination to sway from side to side with every attempted forward motion. The movement was clearly due to a disability, but in those days the disadvantage gave rise to ridicule rather than compassion. People were not deliberately cruel, but seemed to have no qualms about using such hurtful labels.

Brian himself was short of inches but he and his family gained enormously in stature every Bonfire Night. The uncle, who acted as his surrogate father, used to go out and annually spend a fortune on fireworks. An enormously appreciative crowd would gleefully gather for the free show, in bemusement as much as in delight. They marvelled at so much money going up in smoke. Brian's family was granted a kind of unofficial royal status during the proceedings. Among the starbursts, no begrudging eye could be detected as the uplifted heads dutifully honoured their very own Prince Albert.

In 1955, my awareness was elevated from a prince to a king. It was on the entry step to block two that a girl called Elaine regarded me with undisguised

Missing baby – my grandmother and Aunt Kitty stand behind my mother, presumably holding me.

scorn when I admitted to not having heard of a singer called unbelievably – Elvis. My taunter was to maintain her tenuous connection with majesty as she later courted and married a guardsman stationed at the Tower of London. His most important role was the protection of the Crown Jewels.

Although we regarded ourselves as East Enders, our homes were geographically, though fractionally, in the prestigious City of London itself. Not that tourists would have wasted their Kodaks on our premises when the Mansion House, the Bank of England and other more worthy edifices were so close.

The Monument, another famous historical landmark, was not accorded the respect it deserved. This cylindrical edifice was erected on the spot where the Great Fire of London started. It was open to the public and had a circular viewing platform at the top. If one succeeded in climbing the spiral staircase, overcoming breathlessness and vertigo, one looked down directly on passers-by hundreds of feet below. The inevitable boyish antic could not be resisted as my friends and I found ourselves one day the sole occupants of the launching pad. The usual attendant was nowhere in sight and a Niagara Falls of a peeing contest resulted. The ultimate pleasure was to see the unfortunates below looking upwards. They appeared totally mystified by spots of 'rain' falling from a cloudless sky.

One piece of local history still remains etched in the national psyche: the morbid fascination with the never caught, or even identified, Jack the Ripper. In today's East End, countless thrill-seekers pay for the dubious privilege of a guided tour. They appear to relish visiting the spots where his pitiful victims met their horrific deaths, walking in the footsteps of arguably the world's most infamous serial killer. The grim events constituted, for my friends and I, a chilling backdrop to our childhood games, blood having been spilt on the very streets on which we innocently played.

A far less melodramatic history lesson was given to me inadvertently in a park. I was idly watching council workmen cleaning a statue. Once the bird droppings and other encrustations had been removed, the figure of an imposing Victorian male appeared. When the borough's employees left with their tools, I approached the memorial and read the inscription. The man portrayed in stone was General Booth, the founder of the Salvation Army. This brave and determined man conceived the idea of forming a military style organisation to wage war on 'Sin'; of this commodity the East End has never had a shortage.

Learning from books, other than those supplied by school, came courtesy of the Whitechapel Public Library. This stood alongside a far more important beacon of culture, a famous gallery that periodically displayed significant items from the world of art. Perhaps its greatest short-term acquisition was Pablo Picasso's *Guernica*. How sad and fitting that such an iconic painting should be hung in another town that had similarly suffered from bombing.

The Tower of London itself provided at times an alternative playground, and an invaluable history resource. I had read that on its infamous hill Sir Thomas More and many other unfortunates had taken their last look at this world. Nowadays visiting children can learn about the past in more graphic ways. One of the gift shops has on offer executioner's masks and 'bloody' toy axes. A mock severed head could become a best seller for a generation addicted to violent computer games.

My earlier 'hands-on' experience with a real historical artefact was more sober. Along the Tower's embankment overlooking the Pool of London stood several cannon captured by the British Army when Sebastopol fell to it at the end of the Crimean War. They stood on immovable (for us) wooden trucks that we loved to clamber up. Allegedly, one such melted-down weapon provided the metal for the first Victoria Crosses.

We also played Pooh sticks around Traitor's Gate. Dropping little bits of paper or cardboard over the little wall we hoped to see them float through the fearful portcullis. The beefeaters were largely a friendly, chatty and certainly informative bunch. In later life I regretted never having seen a production of Gilbert and Sullivan's *Yeomen of the Guard* on the green sward of the dried-out moat.

The spectacular Gothic Tower Bridge was a source of fascination, above all because in the 1950s its moving bits still actually moved. This allowed even large vessels into the watery part of the City. We loved to stand astride the pavement's great divide, staring down at the narrow split through which a fraction of the river could be seen.

That period of the bridge's story provided a spectacular moment which caught the nation's attention. A bus driver was too late to heed the warning given when the bridge was about to open. With the gap widening before him, he decided to press on with his foot on the accelerator. The land-based vehicle then for a dramatic second took to the air. When paying their fares, those passengers on the top deck could not have anticipated a ride on a Big Dipper! They were not, however, the only ones to fly around London's iconic bridge. It was not unknown for light aircraft and their brave and skilful pilots to fly under the, what could have been, unforgiving ironmongery.

My parents Nancy and Henry twice paid for me to have voyages on the river. A paddle-wheeled steamer, *The Royal Sovereign*, took us all the way down the Thames Estuary to Southend on a memorable summer's day. I relished scaling the steps, looking over the side at the bow wave or the churned water of the wake. The funnel appeared enormous and, when it unexpectedly emitted a great hoot, we all jumped and then laughed at our own fright. The surprisingly permitted view of the engines was a real privilege. I will always remember the all-pervasive smell of oil and the giant metal arms moving rhythmically as they drove the paddle wheels.

The second venture was in 1951 to the Festival of Britain, held on the South Bank. I have one distinct, sad and lasting memory. Henry, after much pleading on my part, had bought me one of the many commemorative badges to mark the event. On our return passage, as I was attempting to pin it to my lapel, it slipped out of my fingers and over the side of the boat. I was devastated to lose something I would have worn with childish pride. Its corroded remains still, I assume, rest on the river's bed. Will some future marine archaeologist find it and puzzle over its nature and how it came to be there?

The Square Mile thus became another part of my playground. During holidays, my friends and I would nip along pavements filled with bowler-hatted gents wielding umbrellas and smart young ladies who were employed in the offices of what still purported to be the world's financial centre. On summer nights and at weekends, the City streets between the concrete canyons emptied and the area became a ghost town.

On both sides of the border that was Middlesex Street (overlooked by our two bedrooms after the Second World War), there were enormous gaps between the buildings. These reminded me of missing teeth, the aerial dentist being the Luftwaffe. The bombsites were great cavities of rubble and debris. Most of the broken homes of those days were the responsibility of Hitler. This dismal playground was a treasure house for the pre-teens. One site was grandiloquently described as 'The Jungle' because of its profusions of weeds. Defying our parents' warnings about jagged bricks and broken glass, we amused ourselves there for hours.

One day an old bedstead was converted into a stretcher during a re-enactment of the recently ended campaign in Malaya. The largest boy, Barry Pack (whose father was unbelievably named – and not nicknamed – Wolfie, making him the butt of many jokes), was accorded the label 'seriously wounded'. He was instructed to lie down on the carrier. Four bearers then raised it but, within seconds, his weight had removed the rusty mesh from the fragile frame. No real major injury was incurred but the story was recounted innumerable times to Barry's discomfiture.

Sometimes on Sundays in the warmer months, my parents treated us to a trip to Hyde Park. Going to a place 'Up West' always held out the prospect of posh spice. A Central Line tube train would take us from Liverpool Street to Marble Arch. Years later, I was to learn that the latter was positioned on the site of Tyburn, in earlier and crueller times the scene of public execution. Thereby hung many a tale!

We entered the park close to Speaker's Corner. As a boy, I viewed it as a peculiar place where loud-voiced somewhat crazy-looking men shouted at jeering crowds who stood before their soap boxes. Later, as a youthful student of history and politics, my perception changed slightly. It clearly had a small paragraph in the story of British democracy and the accompanying tradition of free speech. I came to enjoy the rhetoric of the fanatic even if I didn't always agree with it or understand it. I was impressed with the power of the voices unassisted by microphones and the flow of their words. They seemed to avoid the 'ahs' and 'ers' that punctuated my first efforts at public speaking. They knew the script and rarely fluffed their lines.

The highlight was the heckling. An apt comment from the floor which publicised a self-contradictory point mistakenly made by the orator always got a big laugh. If the victim countered with a telling and perhaps humorous response, the same audience would approve with equal encouragement. I greatly admired the ability to think on one's feet – effective repartee, in my case, being conjured up long after the moment had passed. The range of subjects and points of view enriched the proceedings. 'Workers of the World Unite!', 'Keep Britain White!', 'Africa for the Africans!', 'Prepare to meet thy doom!' Despite the angry words, fights rarely occurred. One solitary policeman, standing at a distance, seemed sufficient to maintain public order. Was the behaviour as good in the House of Commons?

The open-air forum wasn't intended to provide entertainment – that was the purpose of the Easter Parade. My family witnessed some of the last of these innocent fashion and beauty processions which marked the arrival of spring and the celebration of the Christian festival.

Further progress into the park required the crossing of the sandy bridle path. This was sometimes delayed to allow the passage of horse traffic. The riders always seemed to possess an upper-class aura, expressed in the fine cut of their habits, the sparkle of their boots and the upward tilt of their noses. One had the feeling that they were literally looking down on the lower classes.

My spirits were lifted, however, when we reached the Serpentine lake. This stretch of water always appeared on the Pathé newsreels of the day when brave members of its swimming club took to the water during the Christmas holiday (as they still do). Our visits took place when the sun's rays were much stronger. We did not bathe, but hired a rowing boat. Boarding the wobbly craft caused involuntary shrieks – of fear as much as fun. My father's handling of the oars and my mother's of the tiller ropes brought us close to both comedy and tragedy. Henry's instructions, 'Pull the right one . . . now the left one' caused her ribald amusement rather than mutinous anger. She was a Yiddisher Ma – larkin' among the darling buds of May. We often ended up going round in circles and had to suffer the indignity of an amplified voice calling out our number and ordering us to return. The embarrassment was deepened by the patronising looks of the more efficient boat handlers and shore-based laughter. Even the ducks seemed to regard us with a degree of contempt.

My innocent boyish view of the park was altered with the dawning of puberty. 'Adult' information was gleaned from teenage friends and popular Sunday newspapers regarding certain illegal activities which took place within its bounds. From behind the foliage, flashers would emerge to startle unsuspecting ladies. Prostitutes offered sex in the shadows of the trees, and some men used the public lavatory for a particular kind of private practice.

Trafalgar Square was also selected by my parents as a destination for us East End tourists on a sunny Sunday afternoon. I had mixed feelings about this particular venture. I worried about being pestered by the pigeons. The fluttering wings of frenzied feathered friends I found unnerving. A single bird made me wary at close range. When they took off and landed like squadrons of aircraft they seemed a real threat. My biggest fear was that they would shed their 'bomb loads' on a new outfit and my unprotected head.

My father bought the packet of bird food but my sister did the feeding. I could never summon up the courage to allow them to settle on my outstretched hand. I had no wish for the splayed coral feet with their tiny claws to make contact with my flesh.

In contrast the cool spray from the famous fountains was a delight, although I never felt like taking a plunge like brave revellers on New Year's Eve. I was in awe of the huge stone lions that guarded the base of Nelson's Column. So convincing and life-like were these sculptures that they became animated in the occasional childish nightmare. The man at the top seemed a distant figure both in place and time. He clearly had a marvellous view of the country's capital that he so valiantly fought and died for. A pity that the eyes could not see. History later taught me that the great admiral, in reality, was similarly afflicted when it suited his strategic purpose.

Another tourist attraction was St Paul's Cathedral but, on the one occasion I visited it, I was accompanied by some friends and not my parents. It was rare for me to enter a church, but my regard for it stemmed from its place in the history of the Blitz, rather than its religious significance. Our arrival in the cathedral's Whispering Gallery tested my courage as I didn't relish heights. We split into pairs and exchanged little waves across the big divide. In the eerie atmosphere we pretended to be spies and exchange information. From matters of national importance, we drifted on to revelations of personal affairs. I foolishly admitted to liking a plain-looking girl in school. My astonished listener involuntarily exclaimed, 'You fancy ——' and the sweetheart's name went ringing round the chamber.

On reaching ground level, there was some merciless leg-pulling. I hypocritically prayed that night to the Saint in the hope that the ill-advised disclosure would not get back to school. The suspicion that my request would be ignored was unhappily and embarrassingly well-founded.

# two

# First School

My education started at the Canon Barnett Primary in Gunthorpe Street. This was an ill-fitting title as the pupils were mainly Jewish and the august person after whom the school was named was a middle-management figure in the Anglican Church. It bordered Toynbee Hall, built and supported by well-meaning Labourites to assist the adult working class to improve itself.

Canon Barnett was three-tiered with two playgrounds, or rather yards. The one at ground level had open-air toilets, a gift for bold and clambering peeping toms! The other on the roof had protective iron railings and netting to prevent under-age murder or suicide. It also provided a panoramic view. One could follow the course of the sun from Bow Bells to the Tower of London and beyond.

Football and cricket were played on a concrete pitch where the goalposts and wickets were chalked on walls. This led, as season turned to season, into continuous claims of score and dismissal. In reception class, we spent part of the afternoons napping on beds of tubular steel and canvas. Desks were of the hard bench variety and chalkboards and inkwells resulted in fingers continuously stained in blue or white.

The London County Council (LCC) took care of our bodies as well as our minds. Milk was provided for all at break time and a dollop of malt on a large communal spoon for those who looked particularly undernourished. The nit nurse raked hair with a metallic comb that felt like shark's teeth and reeked of disinfectant. The poorly clad received handouts of garments and footwear.

We gave, however, as well as received. Mr Isaac, the senior Jewish teacher, raised funds for the new State of Israel. Chests were puffed out when at assemblies we were informed that our generous contributions had planted another tree in a once-barren land. In the top class, he showed us ciné films

School photograph on a London rooftop. I am the fifth child from the right in the third row.

of a general educational nature on a clicking projector. *Trawling in the North Sea* was interesting but remote. *Coal Mining in South Wales* constituted prime viewing. Boys sniggered and girls giggled as the naked, blackened miners showered on the flickering screen.

Mr Willis, the headmaster, entertained us on Friday afternoons. His piano-playing provided the musical backcloth to rousing renditions of 'The British Grenadiers' and 'There's a Tavern in the Town'. 'Barbara Allen' and 'The Ash Grove' were delivered more tenderly and may well have brought tears to the eyes. Barefooted on the parquet floor, we cavorted under Miss Piggot's direction of 'Sir Roger de Coverley'. It was during one of these innocuous country dance sessions I incurred what turned out to be a nasty little injury. As I sat down on the wooden floor, a large and painful splinter entered the skin below the nail of my thumb. My mother escorted me after school to the London Hospital where it was removed and I was given an anti-tetanus injection. The medical staff informed my mother that in a few cases an adverse reaction took place. If this occurred, a return was necessary to avoid loss of life. As that evening progressed, my temperature soared and my general condition deteriorated. I don't know how far the cry for help extended around the family but it was answered by one of my elder cousins, Louis Overs. I recall being cradled in his muscular arms and driven in his taxi at emergency ambulance speed. We arrived in time and the antidote was successfully administered. Never in the wilder contortions of the jive and twist, both of which provided later dancing delight, did I come so close to death.

Hospitalisation later occurred when a stomach rupture prominent since birth was operated on in the Jewish Hospital in Stepney by the eminent surgeon S.I. Levy. This experience was very unnerving for an edgy child. Although only eight, I was placed in the men's surgical ward. It was on the second floor and overlooked a rare expanse of East End grass, in which large trees were embedded. That night an autumn gale blew. I was very frightened on hearing the sound of huge branches being tormented by high winds for the first time.

As I had had little sleep, the pre-med was superfluous – I am sure I would have been dozy without the soporific. I recall the theatre more clearly than the one at my circumcision. There were gowned and masked figures in rubber gloves. A particularly posh voice instructed me to count 1, 2, 3 . . . My last thought was that it was an odd time for an arithmetic lesson.

On regaining consciousness, my little body was raked by nausea. Never able to be sick with facility, this aftermath of the anaesthetic seemed a refinement of torture. Only on the day after did a semblance of normality return to my shaken state. My attention was drawn to the thick crêpe bandage across the abdominal area that was not unpleasant to the touch. I picked at this benign scab.

Further improvement followed when I discovered a set of earphones behind the struts of the bed. These made available broadcasts on the Light Programme and Home Services of the BBC. I became addicted to *The Archers* and its catchy signature tune. Visiting time involved mixed feelings. I longed to see my mother but feared the bell that signalled a departure rigidly ordered by Sister.

My stay included 5 November, and I was pleased to see the roman candles and rockets in the night sky. I could not, however, shrug off the inevitable feeling of being left out. My mind dwelt on the tremendous fun my friends must have been having during my enforced absence. As my strength and appetite returned, my finicky tastebuds, long spoilt by my mother's cooking, brooked at the hospital food. Like all patients, I felt that the day of my release would never come.

That first Saturday at home was one of my happiest. My father bought a host of weekly comics with his daily paper. The *Beano, Dandy* and *Lion* were avidly read in bed. Dandy the Cat, Desperate Dan, Lord Snooty and his Pals, and my ultimate hero General Jumbo were greeted like long-lost friends, as I leafed through the pages of cartoons and word bubbles. Contentment brimmed over when I listened blissfully to the beguiling songs of a more innocent age.

'The Laughing Policeman', 'The Teddy Bears' Picnic' and 'Home on the Range' informed me that I was back in the comforting world of normality.

Back at Canon Barnett, the mousey Miss Cohen, the lean and spinsterish Miss Silverman and the motherly Mrs James provided a compassionate welcome. The teachers commuted from all over the place. The headmaster lived in the country and cut a dash by choosing a motorbike as his means of conveyance. The other members of staff had the social cachet of suburban homes in semi-detached, privately-owned, establishments. Our Jewish guardians came from the plush areas around the North Circular. Mrs James commuted from distant Romford on the Green Line bus. Her house was a rural idyll with a garden and a potting shed similar to the one seen on *Bill and Ben* on children's television.

Mrs James entertained us with stories of rabbits, squirrels and foxes, none of which we had seen in the flesh. This reminds me that she did provide the class with a peep at her underwear. Her old granny knickers came down to her knees. It was in her class, however, that my interest in geography and history developed. I was allowed to gently spin the globe on her desk; the proviso being that this was done with due care. The flimsy supporting arm of the globe was shaky. I would have been mortified if this innocent activity had turned out to be literally earth-shattering.

The two subjects were not in fact taught officially. Outside the 'Three Rs', general knowledge was included in the lessons when deemed appropriate. Mrs James referred to me as 'our geography expert'. My pride was boundless when she summoned me to the map of Great Britain and ceremoniously handed me her yardstick. My instructions were to point out a particular mountain range, river, sea or city. Returning to my place, fellow pupils would mutter 'map man', half in mockery, half in admiration.

These same whisperers, however, gladly accepted my leadership on excursions across London by bus, underground railway or Shanks's Pony. Our mums and dads did not possess today's paranoia with paedophilia. 'Stranger Danger' was hardly mentioned, and we were thus permitted the freedom of unaccompanied travel from the age of nine. This revelation will probably astonish and horrify many of today's genuinely concerned parents. If there was 'trouble', it was often of our own making.

Visits to Arsenal, Chelsea, Spurs and the lesser London grounds were little expeditions. My encyclopaedic knowledge of buses and their numbers (if changing was involved) and the colour-coded lines of the Underground chart was a requirement of a successful journey. We spent almost an entire day going round and round on the Circle Line, in the comforting position of knowing we would eventually return to the place where we had started. In our case this was Aldgate, sadly one of the targets of a different kind of bomber in the first decade of the new millennium. To pass the time, I'd often be challenged to name the stations in their correct order. Sweets constituted the prize if I got it right and the forfeit if I got it wrong.

After the Festival of Britain in 1951, Battersea Park became London's biggest fairground. For us it was a trans-capital crossing. One return journey involved walking a section of the Thames Embankment as some of our travelling expenses had gone on fair rides. West of Westminster, a thunderstorm struck and forced us to shelter in the porch of an up-market private house. Before we urchins could be shooed off the doorstep by an outraged butler or maid, our upraised thumbs stopped a van. 'East' we chorused through the downpour. 'Hop in the back. I'm going as far as Charing Cross,' responded our saviour who was a chimney sweep. On emerging from the rear of the tradesman's van, a more appropriately named destination would have been Blackfriars. The inevitable sequel tested our mothers' laundering skills to the limit; never in the 1950s did Persil have to 'wash whiter' than this.

Back in the classroom, the world map broadened our knowledge of history as well as geography. We took unashamed satisfaction in observing how much of the world was coloured red, denoting membership of the British Empire. Information about the past often involved telling how our island beat off invaders and then in turn invaded and conquered more of the planet than any previous power. The story was one of pride, not apology. The native peoples were assumed to be delighted with the obvious blessings of Rule Britannia.

Empire Day was an unquestioned cause of celebration. Sir Francis Drake, Sir Walter Raleigh, General Wolfe and Lord Nelson constituted a roll of honour. My gratitude to the Duke of Wellington was boundless for, without him, the country would not possess Waterloo station. Sir Alfred Tennyson's 'Charge of the Light Brigade' was read in awe. In a school library book, I gazed at the splendour of a cavalryman's uniform and his prancing mount. My ten-year-old mind had little knowledge of the horror of the hospital at Scutari, other than that it was dimly illuminated by a lady with an inadequate lamp.

The appalling sacrifices of the First World War were not dwelt upon; only the fact that we had won. As Jewish children, we would be eternally grateful to Great Britain for saving us from horrible Hitler, who we loved to trivialise for having only one testicle. Mindful of living through modern history, I was thankful our country had both the A and H bombs to deter what my father's *Daily Express* called 'the Red Menace' and 'the Yellow Peril'.

The Lord Mayor's Show, seen live on a few occasions, and the Coronation, seen only on TV, were the culminations of Imperial splendour. The marching band of the Royal Marines, uniformed in blue with brilliant white crossbelts were, for me, the highlights of the parades. My young self would have been a willing recruit despite the only musical instrument I possessed being a tin whistle. This had been acquired from a Christmas cracker and on it, sadly, I was never able to produce a single recognisable tune.

## three

# The Lane

The journey to and from school took me through Petticoat Lane, the world-famous street market. It provided sustenance and entertainment. A nucleus of traders occupied the Monday to Friday stalls in Wentworth Street. On Sunday (the big day) stalls also sprouted in the main thoroughfare in Middlesex Street. The patter of the stallholders successfully enticed customers. One purveyor of ladies' dresses used to describe himself not as Christian Dior but as 'Yiddisher Dior'. A coarser male vendor would berate his fellows who hesitated over a purchase with 'There's only one thing that grows in your hand.'

The market had a reputation for dodgy dealing, pick-pocketing and other ways of separating the innocent from their money. The 'three-card trick' con-men were petty rogues who lured in the gullible with bogus punters (their own gang members) posing as ordinary players. Lookouts were posted. They would surreptitiously signal when the law approached. Equipment and personnel would then vanish into the madding crowd. All this seems pretty innocuous when compared to the drug trading and violence which the constabulary have to deal with today.

On the other side of the ledger, the vast majority of the traders worked hard. In the bitterest winters, they stamped numbed feet and blew hot breath on the chilled fingers that emerged from their mittens, and still had the good humour to cheer up the crowd with their own form of clamorous capitalism.

Periodically my friends and I would find employment to augment our pocket money. In the main we laboured cheerfully, but sometimes the merchandise itself could lead to embarrassment. Stanley Chicksand assisted an uncle on his cucumber stall. The phallic vegetable led to teasing, but not too much. 'The Chick' was renowned for a formidable right jab. On one occasion, however, a cheeky little lad yelled out 'Hey Stanley, you are a bigger walley than your cucumbers!' (walley being 'lane-speak' for cucumber and penis). The cowardly boy, already hidden in the crowd, took immediate flight. A seething Stanley vented his pent-up anger on the saleable item he was holding in his fist at that moment. The resulting pulp was clearly of no use to the customers but happily his understanding and generous uncle did not deduct the cost of the crunched cucumber from his nephew's wages.

My own discomfiture revolved around an aunt's shoe stall that sold men's and women's footwear. It was the latter that was to cause my unease. On hot summer Sundays, a glamorous young lady in a flared dress or skirt would require my assistance. As if in *Cinderella*, a fine-looking stockinged foot would be extended for me to fit the high-heeled shoe. It was incredibly difficult from my kneeling position to stop a roving eye from being raised from ankle and shapely calf to intoxicatingly gartered thigh. The skirt was always raised fractionally and deliberately higher than was practically required for the fitting. Although tantalised by her provocative tease, I sadly never stooped to conquer.

Other senses of smell and taste were also in a constant state of arousal. To appease one's hunger, there was a range of ethnic eating to hand. Wafting over the area you could smell the sweet hot doughy bagels and a whole range of delicacies from the delicatessens. Potato latkes, pickled herrings, chicken livers and salt beef sandwiches were staple dishes, many consumed on the hoof. The bakeries topped up the main courses with strudels, cinnamon balls, cheesecakes and Danish pastries for those who had a little in reserve.

As well as the stomach being filled, the mind could be diverted. Street entertainers, though not officially registered like the stallholders, tried to earn a few coppers. The escapologist, tattooed, straight-jacketed and chained, delighted the crowd with his seemingly magical skill. The watchers' appreciation was shown by tossing coins into a cloth cap on the ground.

The Guess-Your-Weight man went for many years unexposed. His gigantic scales were a tremendous eye catcher and crowd puller. The natural human desire to prove a boaster wrong was perhaps the greater attraction. In fact, he proved to be infallible within his own set limit of 4lbs. There was never a shortage of volunteers of all shapes and sizes. They were ever-ready to part with their pennies for what our present age might regard as a public humiliation. Before mounting the apparatus, they were subjected to hands-on assessment which covered considerable areas of their bodies. The audience relished and laughed at this examination. The Guess-Your-Weight man, however, gave a very convincing impression of taking the whole activity seriously. No flicker of a smile or any other sign of pleasure was detectable.

To the surprise of his fellow hawkers and his paying customers, the Guess-Your-Weight man came to an abrupt end. After years of uninterrupted appearances, one Sunday morning he did not show up. Without the gigantic scales, the lane appeared to have a missing tooth. Man and machine were never seen again. A month after his finale, the *News of the World* provided the answer to the mystery. In a West London magistrates court, the Guess-Your-Weight man had been fined £2 . . . for persistent and improper groping.

My particular favourite in the lane wore a stunning headdress of gaily coloured ostrich plumes atop a bejewelled body swathed in flowing robes above open sandals. It was a he and not a she. Prince Monolulu was a racing tipster. The authenticity of his title was open to debate, but this only added to the charisma of this coffee-coloured con-man allegedly from the 'Dark Continent'. He would summon his tribe of admirers with his much celebrated war cry, 'I gotta horse!' The 'Prince' had a sublime patter. He claimed his invaluable information was granted to him in the marble halls of the great and the good. In these stately homes, he was the most honoured of guests, and his hosts could not wait to shower him with updates on the well-being of their pampered thoroughbreds.

Nevertheless, despite being on the closest of terms with peers of the realm and the Chief Rabbi (this was added in subtle deference to the ethnicity of the area), he was at heart a man of the people. This explained his presence in the lane. Like another great philosopher, Karl Marx, he believed sincerely in the redistribution of wealth. Thus, for a mere sixpence, anyone could buy a folded note, inside which was inscribed the name of a 'certainty' for a specific race on the following week's racing calendar. Should any doubter question his integrity, he would stand on that very spot at the same time the following week and return, in the most unlikely event of defeat, the lost outlay of those who had shown faith.

Prince Monolulu claimed that in 1953 he received an official gilt-edged invitation to the crowning of the new young and beautiful queen. This, he further stated, enabled him to ride in one of the coronation coaches. No witness was ever found to substantiate these boasts. In total contrast, a more credible rumour was circulated. It transpired that, on the momentous day, the Prince was spotted heading for Uxbridge on a Green Line bus. He was wearing shaded glasses and his feathers had a decided droop.

Monolulu was not the only charlatan to beguile the ears of a public ever-willing to listen to a tall story. 'Doctor' Alfie Carl held no qualification that would have been acknowledged by any reputable teaching hospital. Nevertheless, hanging from his stall were a number of framed certificates testifying to his ability as a medical practitioner. To give his act even more credibility, he wore a long, white linen coat that would have graced the wards at the nearby London Hospital. Round his neck dangled a stethoscope, and from his top pocket protruded an impressive array of pens. Slightly above these, as a final dramatic touch, one's eye was drawn to a spatula.

His much-vaunted patent medicine was a cure for infected throats and chests. It was a pink substance bottled in small glass containers and cost patrons no more than a shilling. Alfie claimed that the great Alexander Fleming had praised its healing qualities. Its inventor couldn't disclose the ingredients of the mixture as he feared his jealous rivals would manufacture it under another name – the concoction was in fact nothing but ground-down cough candy. This was purchased every Friday night by my cousin Dickie from a local sweet shop. Not only did my relative act as Alfie's secret buyer, but he furthered his elementary knowledge of science as the alchemist's apprentice. Dickie experimented in private. He took several doses of Alfie's cure and discovered that its only value was as a laxative.

Alfie's brother Maxi was also in the business of private health care. How proud their aged Jewish mother must have been to have two doctors in the family. What difference did it make if their premises were in Wentworth Street and not Harley Street?

Maxi's specialism was in a lower part of the body to that of his brother – the curing of corns. His spiel required the presence of a stooge. Sitting uncomfortably and self-consciously beside him on a large wooden chair was a barefooted man displaying tortured toes. This side-kick came from the bottom and cheapest end of the labour market, being a tramp enticed out of the local Salvation Army hostel by the jingle of Maxi's money. After a lengthy build-up about the origin and nature of the offending pieces of hardened flesh, Maxi came to a sudden and very effective climax. With a theatrical flourish he drew an open razor from an inside pocket, and waved it in front of the horrified hobo. After the last gasp had subsided, Maxi carefully closed the blade and declared that he had reconsidered and that surgery was not necessary. Although operations were suspended and the air filled with a mixture of disappointment and relief, Alfie maintained control of his audience.

For the swift and painless removal of corns, he would now show what was required. Like a matador, he then whipped a green cloth off the main body of his stall to reveal an artistic pyramid of bottles containing a purple substance. This unique unguent would cost sufferers a mere half-crown. Dickie was also associated with this enterprise. He claimed that in summer he used the elixir for hardening his cricket bat.

Maxi's rather callous treatment of his assistant was somewhat typical of a certain East Ender attitude towards vagabonds. The wealthy may have casually conferred their charity, and some members of the middle class, perhaps with a religious impetus, may have administered and staffed hostels either as paid employees or volunteers, but in the ranks of the working class, the people closest to the down-and-outs in the social hierarchy, there was little tolerance or compassion. The prevalent attitude was more like one of contempt.

The less affluent fought a constant material battle to retain a little dignity and self-respect. They worked to put roofs over the heads of their children and food in their mouths. The bailiff knocking at the door was a sound they were determined to avoid, as was the sight of an empty larder. The policy towards poverty was one of 'never surrender'. Tramps, on the other hand, had clearly raised the white flag. Such defeatism was unacceptable. Those who indulged in it were not deserving of any sympathy. This feeling towards those who appeared to wallow in their own filth was passed down from parents to kids. The tramps (or dossers, as they would often be called) could be seen shuffling along the street, brewing up on derelict sites, sleeping in shop doorways or congregating on tiny areas of public grass that the area retained.

One such sward stood beside Spitalfields Church. My friends and I labelled it 'Itchy Park' for the inmates were frequently spotted scratching their unkempt bodies. The title expressed our physical revulsion for these miserable looking men and sometimes women. They seemed like dirty, oversized rag dolls. We never went close enough to smell them. If we saw a member of this underclass and feared an approach, we readily pelted him with discarded rotting vegetables and fruit. We had no pangs of conscience or remorse; they deserved what they got. This attitude and consequent treatment was a far cry from the popularity of the piano-playing tramp in the 1950s West End musical hit *Salad Days*. It was even further away from the future hit song 'Streets of London'.

'Shelter' was a building that protected people from air raids, not an organisation to help the homeless and vendors of the *Big Issue*. We had no interest in the physical ailments with which they appeared to be afflicted. Their poor mental health, evidenced by talking to themselves or outbursts of anger against a lamp-post, induced fear or provided entertainment and a deranged vagrant was considered fair game. The only question was how fast could you run after you had taunted him? One was dubbed 'Cocoa' after layers of encrusted dirt on his face and hands had turned a white man seemingly into a brown one. One of the biggest insults that we hurled at each other was to call a boy 'Cocoa'. This indicated what was thought of his appearance and aroma.

A sleeping tramp in the days before Bonfire Night could be a target for a specific attack. The biggest laugh resulted from an exploding banger being thrown at such a figure. Firing a rocket from a milk bottle laid on its side was tempting, but risky. If the aim was bad, the misdirected missile could hit an innocent party or damage property – drawing the law's attention to our conduct was thought inadvisable.

My mother and I once passed a tramp sitting with his back to the railings of Itchy Park. He was drinking from a tin can. 'What must be happening in his stomach?' she asked rhetorically. She was referring to his inability to afford alcohol. He was pouring methylated spirit down his throat. The tramp's toast could not have been 'Good Health'. I speculated what would happen if a spark from a discarded 'dog-end' made contact with the liquid. Would he transform into a human flame-thrower? I further wondered how long such beggars could be expected to live and what happened to the corpses when they died. One day I witnessed the removal of such a body by employees of the local council. A sadly young and indifferent mind viewed the matter as an example of rubbish collection.

Two of my uncles ran the business of erecting the stalls for the market from 4.00 a.m. on Sunday morning with a batch of paid employees. My boyhood sleep was far deeper than it is at present and the crashes and cries from the street two storeys below never disturbed my unconscious state. Late on Sunday afternoon, they had the job of dismantling everything. By early evening amazingly all the squashed fruit and vegetables and other detritus of the market would be cleared. The number 78 buses could then resume their passage linking Aldgate with Liverpool Street station.

On Saturday, quiet descended on the Lane as all the inhabitants were supposed to observe the Jewish Sabbath. The religious worshipped conventionally in the synagogue. Those who idolised Spurs and Arsenal expressed their piety at White Hart Lane and Highbury.

# four

# Famous Firms

The area housed a number of businesses that achieved localised celebrity and, in one particular case, national recognition. At the southern end of Goulston Street was the enormous bulk of the Brooke Bond tea building. The 1950s witnessed the last significant use of horse-drawn vehicles and this firm used some magnificent beasts to pull their delivery carts. These huge horses were beautifully groomed and accoutred. One remembers the jingle of the shiny harness, the sleek coats and manes and shaggy fetlocks. On the high seat at the front of the cart sat the driver in uniformed splendour. These animal lovers would guide their charges with gentle and sensitive handling of the long reins. They were equipped with lengthy whips. If used, the intended encouragement or admonishment was delivered only with the lightest of flicks and an affectionate 'Giddy up'. I never witnessed the whip used in anger. If the horses were to be killed, it would have been by kindness rather than cruelty. Their handlers fed them apple cores and sundry other morsels of fruit and veg.

We were sometimes allowed to stroke them and, if brave enough, rub their noses and pop a peppermint into their mouths. The opportunity to get up on the cart never presented itself, much to our sorrow. We were of the generation that worshipped Westerns, riveted by John Wayne in *Stagecoach*, Bob Hope in *Paleface* and Doris Day in *Calamity Jane*. These classics had gripping action scenes involving flying horse-pulled carriages. What a *High Noon* we would have had driving a Deadwood Stage down Aldgate High Street!

There was, however, a far less glamorous and romantic contact with our four-legged friends. These enormous creatures left correspondingly large 'visiting cards'. Brown mud-coloured mounds were deposited on the street where we frequently played and the task of picking a trapped ball out of the pile was not a popular activity. An ill-considered sliding tackle during a game of football did nothing for the appearance of one's short trousers, thigh or socks, and the addition to the washing pile was not popular with our mothers. At night, one could inadvertently take an innocent and misguided step into the 'proverbial'.

As the age of television moved into the field of commercialisation, Brooke Bond was to provide the nation's viewers with one of the most memorable of the early advertisements. The almost human chimpanzees that starred in the PG Tips tea party were hugely popular.

On the junction of Goulston Street and Aldgate High Street stood the legendary Tubby Isaacs jellied eel stall. The naming was somewhat ironic. A Jewish title directly linked with non-kosher food was like sighting a pork sausage in a synagogue! The huge wriggly worms were a long-standing favourite with cockneys. There were many Jews, however, who found Tubby's forbidden food irresistible. They brazenly sampled the various delicacies in full public view. Cockles and mussels were as popular as on the Dublin streets of the Catholic Molly Malone.

I had a rather ambivalent attitude to the stall. Most of its displayed items left me as cold as the ice they rested on and my nostrils took no delight in the aroma which could carry 100 yards down the street with an unfavourable wind. The live and slithery eels made my flesh creep. The discarded disembodied heads and the spat-out bones which found their way into the gutter made me feel sick and featured in my childhood nightmares. Eventually, when I plucked up courage to taste the contents of my father's proffered bowl, I found that I enjoyed the vinegar-soaked jelly which accompanied the eel and I became particularly partial to the chunks of white bread as well.

Bloom's kosher restaurant was situated close to the Whitechapel Art Gallery. Spotless white linen cloths adorned the tables while waiters and not waitresses provided a silver service. I never discovered if this was of any religious significance. The speciality of the house was salt beef. This could be purchased in sandwich form at the counter (I don't recall the words 'take-away' being used). Alternatively, you could book a table and eat it in style. Besides the meat, the favourite vegetables were potato latkes. In the preparation of the beef, saltpetre was used and could have accounted for the not unpleasant explosion in the mouth. The spicy and oily latke accounted for many an expanded waistline.

The dessert menu contained, in my case, only one must-have item – the lockshen pudding. It was a sweet pasta pudding made with eggs and cinnamon, studded with sultanas and yellow in colour. Its deliciously crusty top was powdered with sugar. The only drawback was the no-cream regulation. In

Jewish dietary law, milk and meat are not a favoured combination within the same meal. The no-milk rule had a bearing on the end of the meal. The standard drink was lemon tea. I was told this contained health-giving qualities, but it still took three spoonfuls of sugar to make the medicine go down. Orthodox Jews ate in full regalia. Many men wore kippahs which were very similar to the little piece of head-covering often worn by the Pope . . . oi vey!

I can't recall my mother and father being anything other than bare-headed. Mr Bloom operated a tolerant regime, seemingly because a broad clientele put a smile on the face of his accountant. I was never aware, however, of any gentile patrons, for whom the bill of fare would have held little appeal. The contrast with today is noticeable. The bagel can be bought in most supermarkets in this part of Christendom.

The 1950s witnessed the end of many small businesses that had flourished for many years. Woods was a large grocer in Aldgate High Street, the sights and smells of which still linger in the memory. I can recall my mother leading me into this emporium clutching a ration card in her other hand. The air was filled with a beguiling mixture of aromas, provided by rashers of bacon , hunks of cheese and coffee beans. The sawdust underfoot added to the atmosphere. Its purpose was to soak up unpleasant and dangerous spillages and prevent customers taking nasty tumbles with laden shopping bags. If an accident were to occur, it was most unlikely, in those days, that Mr Woods would have received a solicitor's letter. The thought of suing would not have entered anyone's head.

In Middlesex Street, Evan's Dairy caused me to speculate what was a Welshman doing among the Hebrews? Evan rarely spoke but, when he did, he had a wonderfully deep voice. On one occasion, I heard him chastise an assistant and an almighty sound echoed round the room, the concrete floor and bare walls lending power to the volume. My childish imagination envisaged the milk curdling inside the iron churns!

A cobbler's shop could be found in Toynbee Street. The craftsman working inside was a magnet for much boyhood window gazing – this aproned figure would fascinate his young onlookers with his skilled shaping of the leather soles and heels. His pièce de résistance was the manner in which he held the tiny nails between his lips prior to hammering them rapidly into the awaiting shoe. I used to wonder if he ever swallowed a nail in a moment of forgetfulness. What effect would that have had on his stomach? The cruder of my friends wondered how painful a thin piece of metal could be when it eventually made its exit.

The 1950s also saw the passing of the old street service providers. These included the knife grinder whose circulating stone wheel sent tiny sparks flying.

When a blade made contact with the revolving sharpener, a grating squeal set the teeth on edge and sent a shiver down the spine. Shoe-shine boys positioned themselves in and around railway stations. Customers placed one foot at a time on an angled platform while the cleaner sat astride a small stool. He then polished and buffed until he could see his own reflection in the leather.

In winter, one of the most welcome vendors was the man who pedalled a tricycle, on the front of which was a basket containing burning coal on which chestnuts were roasted. These delicious treats were then sold in small paper bags. Our frozen fingers got as much pleasure from holding them as our stomachs did from eating them.

# five

# Train-Spotting

It was in the massive arcade of Liverpool Street station that my boyhood hobby of train-spotting began. Here the great locomotives arrived from, and departed for, the East of England. In the summer, young passengers set off with bucket and spade to Clacton. I can recall long lines of National Servicemen awaiting departure for Colchester with rifle and kitbag. Their officers would marshal them wearing Sam Browne belts, peaked caps and leather gloves. Under their arms they carried swagger sticks.

The steam engines themselves with their numbers and names provided greater interest. Once sighted, the spotter underlined them in his manual published by Ian Allan. The most impressive class for me was the 'Britannia'. As a 'Brit' rounded the curve into the station, I strained to see whether it was one that I had not set eyes on before. Names from British history and literature were revealed (and learned) when the inscription on the nameplate could be read: *Alfred the Great*, *The Black Prince*, *William Shakespeare*, *John Milton* and *Robert Burns* were among those I underlined in my book.

When allowed to venture further afield, I visited King's Cross. There I spied 'streaks' of which *The Mallard* was the most famous. My horizons were imperially widened by engines such as *The Union of South Africa* and *The Dominion of Canada*. At school, I proudly sported the spotters' club badge without any fear of ridicule. Apart from succumbing to the temptation of planting copper coins on the line, it was the most innocent of pastimes.

My greatest thrill, however, was to be invited one day into the cab of an engine with the driver and fireman. I'm not sure that even in those less-regulated times that this was strictly legal, but I certainly was never going to raise the matter with my benefactors. The hissing beauty had stood stationary for some time. I had been looking up adoringly from Liverpool Street's platform 3 when the peak-capped engineer looked down.

'Permission to come aboard,' he declared to my astonishment. Unassisted, I clambered up the blackened steps and entered the holy of holies. Around me was a paraphernalia of levers, pulleys, buttons, gauges, wheels, dials and brake handles.

'Don't stand there gawping. Do something useful!' ordered my instructor who, without any ceremony, thrust a shovel into my hands. I then deposited two loads of best Welsh coal into the furnace of the boiler.

The smell of steam returns occasionally and nostalgically to delight my nostrils and recapture those magic moments. Re-runs of steam engines still draw bands of devoted 'anoraks' from my generation. Digital cameras now record contemporary tributes to Victorian science. In the 1950s, we happily settled for the black and white photos taken by a Box Brownie.

Since semi-retirement in 2002, I have become a modest collector of models of the great engines of my childhood. A five-shelved wooden cabinet displays the purchases I've made from toy fairs across my region. They are brought home in attractive boxes still bearing the impressive logos of Hornby and Tri-ang. Sadly, as Britain is no longer 'the Workshop of the World', the packaging declares that the enclosed items are made in China. I commissioned a local artist to manufacture and inscribe a sign bearing the legend 'Hazlemere Halt' although no train ever ran through the middle of my house. As an extra self-indulgence, I asked for the lettering to be in the cream and brown livery of the old Great Western Railway. This rests on top of the cabinet.

In a corner of my local football team's training ground, some hard working enthusiasts run and maintain a figure of eight sit-upon model railway. It has a quaint platform and bridge. During the summer months, my grandchildren, Megan, Jamie and Josh and I buy our yellow (adult) and pink (child) tickets and enjoy countless rides. It is a charming experience for us all, but I suspect that the passenger who gains the greatest pleasure is the most senior.

# six

# *Hebrew*

Train-spotting was a personal choice. Hebrew lessons were not. In Brick Lane there was a synagogue with a chaider (school) attached. At my mother's insistence, I had to attend this school on a couple of evenings a week from the age of ten. My parents did not have any real religious feelings, but to let me off would have led to an unacceptable loss of face within the community; I, like many others, was a sacrificial lamb of tradition. I simply resented early winter evenings away from the increasing number of children's TV programmes including Western heroes like *The Lone Ranger* and *The Cisco Kid*. In summer, I looked through the windows at the children of non-believers playing happily in the streets.

Few of the Hebrew teachers impressed me. They were not professional rabbis but taught at the chaider after their day jobs. The two Mr Goldsteins constituted the main misery and fuelled my resentment. The short fat one was a chicken plucker. When he came close to suspecting inattention or worse, he carried a vicious little stick in his hands. Under his fingernails was the evidence of 'fowl deeds'. He also bought with him an unpleasant whiff of the slaughterhouse where the creatures were decapitated. The other Mr Goldstein, though less melodramatic in appearance, was more sinister. Behind pebble glasses, supercilious eyes looked down on lesser brains who were experiencing difficulty with the archaic language. He continually boasted of the extent of his Sabbath observance and any violation of it on our part would have horrified him. He probably would have had a fit of apoplexy had he overheard one of the boy's confession that on Yom Kippur, the Day of Atonement, he had discovered the pleasures of masturbation.

I did retain respect, however, for one of their number. Mr Linden instructed us in Jewish history. He told his Biblical tales with gusto, the chosen people always triumphing in the end with the help of the Almighty. God's name was never spoken, and I often wondered whether the entire building would crash down on our heads should someone utter it unthinkingly. This possibility troubled me, particularly during the year I was taught on the ground floor.

The journey to and from the chaider had some points of wider theological interest. Ironically, by far the most impressive landmark was the Anglican bulk of Nicholas Hawksmoor's masterpiece, Christ Church, Spitalfields. In the pea-souper fogs of the early 1950s, its white walls provided helpful guidelines to those who had rejected Christ and could not see the light.

Christchurch School, a Catholic establishment, held out menace rather than succour. Lone Hebrew scholars passing its railings could received verbal and physical abuse from the young students.

We strayed from the sacred, Sabbath path in many ways. There was, for example, our joyful attendance at the heathen temple called the Mayfair. This was a well known flea-pit, or cinema, where we shared the delights of the Saturday morning pictures with thousands of non-Jewish kids across the country. The films were mainly from far-away America, providing us with a host of new secular and spectacular heroes to worship including cowboys such as Hop-Along Cassidy and Roy Rogers.

Superman was a link to the present day, being the forerunner of future super heroes. His death-defying feats against a host of villains always concluded with a cliff-hanger. At the end of each weekly episode, our hero would appear to have run out of options for escape. We were compelled to return the following week to see how disaster was inevitably avoided. The dramatic formula was certainly good for the box office. In contrast to the Westerns and adventure films, the comedy came from the slapstick of Laurel and Hardy and any number of cartoon characters, including Mickey Mouse and Bugs Bunny in 'Technicolor'!

The films themselves were only part of the entertainment. The cinema had an upstairs or balcony. If you obtained a seat in this area, and particularly one in the front row, you were provided with a perfect launch platform. From this vantage point, you could propel peanuts, popcorn, hard-boiled sweets and chewing gum that had lost its flavour at the heads of the kids below. The military advantage of this high ground was only sacrificed when the beam of the usherette's torch picked out the culprits. The manager would be summoned, resulting in (possibly permanent) expulsion from the promised land. The rabbis would join the Rank Organisation in approving of a punishment which was well suited to the breaking of the eleventh commandment; thou shall not be found out!

There was also the sense that, when one strayed outside the obvious Jewish areas, anti-Semitism could come into play. Our noses recognised the smell.

At primary school, I acquired my first pair of studded boots. I was desperate to wear them but they were for use on grass pitches and Victoria Park was several miles away from our hard-surfaced streets. To get there, the number 8 bus had to pass through Bethnal Green, rumoured to be a recruiting ground for fascism. Caution decreed that my playmates and I should sit on the lower deck, near the safety of the bus crew. I have to report that no fascists made themselves known to us! We assumed that we were recognisably Jewish even though we did not wear the garments of the Orthodox. Long black gabardine coats and broad-brimmed felt hats, with ringlets dangling down the side of pale faces, were more visible in Stamford Hill and in Golders (Goldberg's) Green than in Aldgate.

Once at the park, we would place jackets and jerseys on the grass to serve as the absent goalposts before proceeding with the game. Non-Jewish kids played nearby in identical fashion but we never received an invitation to play with them and, being ignored, never dared to ask them to play with us either.

At the age of thirteen, I was sent for a soccer trial for the East London district team. I was accompanied by the fair-haired Terry Duncan who lived outside our normal school catchment area in Shadwell. I never discovered why he opted to receive his secondary education in the 'Ghetto'. He was a fine footballer and a loyal friend. We arrived at the place for the trial to discover that most of the hopefuls had already arrived. One greeted us with an insulting and supposedly intimidating challenge, 'Here comes Terry the Jewboy.' It got one laugh, several smirks and a few lowered eyes. Terry told our tormentor to 'piss off', and gave me a philosophical shrug.

Initially, I was uncertain whether the two P.E. teachers might be similarly biased against me. Would one of the 'chosen people' be chosen? In the event, I was selected. That perhaps was the best response to the unwelcoming fellow trialist, who was in fact to receive the 'thumbs down'. Was that my 'pound of flesh'?

The relationship between Jews and Christians seldom fails to come up with the unexpected. Many years ago, a cousin's cousin on my father's side of the family created a mini sensation when he married the early 1960s Jewish pop star Helen Shapiro. Apart from her records such as '(Please) Don't Treat Me Like a Child', 'You Don't Know', 'Walking Back to Happiness' and 'Tell Me What He Said' rising high in the charts, she had the enviable distinction of topping the bill of a nationwide tour on which the Beatles were one of the supporting acts. More recently, I was intrigued to read in my local Buckinghamshire newspaper that she belongs to a group of Jews who believe that Jesus is the Messiah.

In 2007, my blonde wife Susan and I paid our first visit to Eilat in Israel. We were the last passengers to be dropped off by the mini-bus driver. Our hotel was some way from the promenade where our fellow tourists had been deposited at the upmarket hotels catering for an international clientele. During our week stay, we only had verbal communication with a few members of the not very co-operative staff. None of our fellow Israeli guests uttered a single word or even looked us in the eye. It was not the 'homecoming' I'd expected. It was with relief that we joined a coach excursion to Jerusalem carrying large numbers of chatty Brits. Our initial impression of the country was counterbalanced by the charm of our Israeli guide who displayed a sardonic Jewish sense of humour. A gas fitter from Leeds asked him about the differences between the many Jewish festivals. He replied that basically all Jewish festivals were the same; 'You try to kill us . . . we survive . . . we eat.'

The Israeli guide's humour reminds me of an earlier take on the two religions and, to an extent, their accompanying lifestyles. In the late 1990s, my wife and I were invited out by two non-Jewish friends to the London Palladium. Sue and Tony Miles had acquired complimentary tickets for a performance of *The Young Jewish Entertainer of the Year Show*. The seats came courtesy of another friend who was choreographing part of the performance. The 'house' was full. As the first act neared its conclusion, a thirsty Tony nudged me. In an undertone, he suggested that we made an early and quick dash for the bar in order to avoid the usual stampede. I turned towards him and remarked that there was no need to rush as he would be able to down as many pints of beer, and Sue as many glasses of wine, as they wished in the allotted time. A doubtful expression appeared on his perspiring face. When the house lights went up, we were greeted with the sight of an audience largely remaining seated. On many laps appeared greaseproof wrapped picnics containing vast amounts of food from the Jewish delicatessens situated in the area. Any number of smoked salmon and cream cheese bagels was then consumed. Tony's eventual walk to the bar was that of the lonely. He and the staff behind the counter looked at each other in bewilderment. A strong link between the Jewish community and the current craze of binge drinking has not been established.

# seven

# Bar Mitzvah

My mother insisted on back-up. The midweek input of religion was supported by compulsory attendance on Saturdays at the Sandy's Row Synagogue, which in the 1970s featured in the BBC production of Jack Rosenthal's *Bar Mitzvah Boy*. My mentor, Rabbi Newman, played himself in a brief scene in this television drama.

Between those hallowed walls one Saturday in October 1957, I nominally attained the status of manhood. The event drew a crowd as a host of relatives, many of them wayward worshippers, gathered to witness proceedings. On the following day, Stoke Newington Town Hall was hired with me as the centre of attention. Snowy white tablecloths, laden with bowls of fruit and bottles of wine, provided the basis of the banquet. Beer and spirits were on the house although few men indulged, in total contrast to Anglo celebrations. The men were in their rented Moss Bros dinner jackets, the ladies were coiffured and perfumed to the nines. A twelve-piece band and a red-coated and magnificently moustachioed master of ceremonies added sound and colour. I was the principal after-dinner speaker and sat down to applause. In all honesty, the proceedings made me squirm a little. The cost was the result of years of scrimping and saving by my hard-pressed parents, and I felt undeserving. All I had achieved was to reach my thirteenth year and to memorise some hieroglyphics from the Torah.

This rite of passage, many years later, still leaves me uneasy. It's the ambivalence of being part and not part of one's origins. On the one hand, I am unable, indeed unwilling, to deny my roots. On the other, the certainties of institutionalised religion and its loudest and most arrogant protagonists still fail to convince.

A padded photograph album, with the lettering in embossed gold leaf, provides a lasting memory. My mother derived enormous satisfaction as

Bar Mitzvah banquet with me seated between my mother and father. Uncle Morris stands at the microphone.

Belle of the Ball. I hope too that my father, as he was handed the bill on that long-ago Sunday night in the emptying hall, believed that it was worth it. In all the black and white photographs in which he appears, a beaming and apparently unforced smile lights up his fortyish face. The menu has long gone, but the present of a riding whip tie pin with two horses' heads remains in a little satin-lined box, later to be joined by my university cufflinks.

Synagogue attendance then fell away dramatically. Only subsequent family Bar Mitzvahs and weddings required it. The sad attendance at funerals took place elsewhere – in cemetery chapels in the various burial grounds around the city's outskirts. The starkness of Jewish funerals comes as a shock to the uninitiated. There are no uplifting hymns – only mournful chants and responses. The absence of flowers deprives the bereaved of colour and scent.

The severe nature of the Jewish disposal of the dead is highlighted by contrast with other faiths. Some decades after my Bar Mitzvah, the demographic nature of our area began to change. Asian communities equalled and then outnumbered the indigenous Jews. Phoebe, a distant relation by marriage, was watching a Sikh funeral procession in honour of a departed elder. Phoebe was a deliciously comic character with a witty turn of phrase. She was curious and chatty, and critics might have labelled her a nosey-parker. The smiling mourners were ornately dressed in a host of colourful garments. There was a loud musical accompaniment of bells and chimes. This gave a festive air to what in other religions (and certainly in Judaism) would have been at best a sad and, at worst, a grim proceeding. Phoebe was captivated by the apparent joyous nature of the event. So moved was she that tears dripped down her fleshy cheeks. A solicitous Asian man witnessed what he took to be her discomfiture and politely asked if she needed assistance. Phoebe suppressed a snuffle and declined his kind offer, informing him that the funeral was a delight. She then added, well naturedly but perhaps ill advisedly, 'You know, I'd rather attend three of yours than one of ours.'

# eight

# The Racing Page

O ne reason for not turning the pages of the Old Testament was that I now became totally preoccupied with reading those in the 'Form Book', the racing man's bible. My paternal grandfather's youthful enthusiasm for cigar-making (his first job) faded shortly after the First World War. A major career change brought him to the bookmaking business – turf accounting, not publishing. In those far off days, on-course betting was the only form of betting to meet with official approval. Men with loud voices and even louder checked suits stood on wooden stools beside display boards, shouting the odds. On their metal 'joint' was an 'odd', a large leather satchel which contained the betting notes of the punters. Above it, was a tin tray containing their silver. On the bag was painted the name of the firm. The one my ancestor purchased carried the illustrious title of Captain Webb, the first man to swim the English Channel. The unknown vendor's title was lopped off and replaced by his own name, George.

My first visit to the races must have been when I was about four years old. I remember being held up so that I could catch a fleeting glimpse of the multi-coloured silk jackets and caps of the jockeys. I didn't see much of their mounts, except their ears.

My new-found freedom after my Bar Mitzvah enabled me to accompany the firm on a regular Saturday basis. Its elders were my grandfather (the bookie) and his brother Put (an unusual nickname that puzzled me although I never queried its origin or derivation). Put was one of the two tic-tacs. The other was my father's brother Phil who bore a strong resemblance to the gambling mad Sergeant Bilko of TV fame. Phil's nickname, however, was 'Tiptoes' because of his comical manner of bouncing on his feet as he walked. My father, who had a natural gift for figures, was the clerk. His job was to enter bets in the ledger at lightning speed and, in addition, provide instant updates on projected profit and loss. This pre-computerised data would be passed on to my grandfather who would make the adjustments according to how much capital was to hand that day.

Contrary to popular belief, most bookies struggled to earn even a modest living – particularly in winter due to ice, snow, fog or waterlogged courses. Even when the weather allowed racing to take place, fewer people chose to brave the wintry conditions. I never knew a bookie who owned a Rolls-Royce or took holidays in the Caribbean. In fact, I doubt whether many of them could have put their finger on the West Indies in the atlas at the public library. Again, contrary to preconceived opinions, few bookies ran off with the money, the reverse being more often the case. Most had little pocket books listing punters' names and the amounts they owed and, in many cases, never paid. It was not a thriving business. One of my cousins often remarked about my father, 'He was the only man I knew who lived on his losses.' The winters of the late 1950s and early '60s passed with the shadow of debt hanging over us. I breathed a sigh of relief when my father informed me each summer that 'the Firm' was once again in the black.

Among the almost impoverished racecourse characters, Monty and Bernie Levine fell into the category of real strugglers. They were also the 'Silver Ring's' equivalent of Morecambe and Wise. Lancastrian brothers from a Jewish area of Manchester (the poorer one), they had a strong amateur dramatic background. As a double act, they entertained fellow passengers on otherwise humdrum journeys to and from the tracks of the south-east of England.

They conducted their largely unsuccessful business under the alliterative name of 'Jolly Joe', and lived up to the description as the punters relished their wisecracks even when they were the victims of their barbs.

From the mid-1950s to the mid-1960s, Monty acted as the front man on the stool and Bernie fulfilled the role of the backroom boy, recording the incoming bets in the ledger. Eventually, after one of the longest of their losing runs, Monty quit and looked around for a proper job, or at least one that was better paid.

The straw that broke the camel's back came on a bleak December Saturday afternoon at Sandown Park when a succession of favourites passed the winning post in first place. As soon as the first popular punters' choice crossed the line, Monty tentatively approached the most sympathetic of his fellow bookmakers for a small and temporary loan. The money was needed to pay the queue of smiling customers in front of his stand. The 'Form Book' continued to guide its readers to wager successfully. Monty's begging bowl was filled throughout the afternoon by his colleagues. By the time the last favourite had won, his fellow bookmakers, who themselves had had a disastrous day, called a halt to the lending. The man who had misplaced his trust in horses was about to be thrown to the dogs. Crestfallen, Monty slowly mounted his stall and produced from his otherwise empty pocket a little notebook and the stub of a pencil. He was about to inscribe the names and addresses of the now aware and angry punters who would only be paid in the distant and uncertain future.

The brothers were duty-bound to do this as failure meant immediate withdrawal of their trading licence by the racecourse authorities. In fact, it was only the presence of an official and two constables that prevented justice being carried out on the spot in the form of a lynching. As one cruel wit passed the scene, he shouted a sarcastic request to the besieged brothers, 'Oi, Eric and Ernie! Can you put my name down on your Christmas card list?' Bernie surprisingly survived the Sandown showdown and he single-handedly led the resurrected enterprise once the outstanding debts had been cleared. As leading man, he went on to impress his forgiving fellow bookies with a string of attractive girlfriends. He had a marriage of sorts but, like Captain Mainwaring's wife in *Dad's Army*, Mrs Bernie was never seen by me – not on a racecourse at least. What further impressed his co-workers was that, at 5ft 3in, with a balding head and a pot belly, he pulled birds who towered over him. They usually came from the theatrical world and were believed to be 'good sports'. Ribald remarks abounded as reference was made to Bernie needing a leg-up to get mounted. When a new quiz game called *The Golden Shot* appeared on TV, he became known as 'Bernie the Bolt'. On arriving at Lingfield Park one day with a pronounced limp, his 6ft playmate was suspected of excessive use of the whip.

Racing was a Runyonesque world of shady but interesting characters. One-armed Lou could count pound notes and shuffle a pack of cards as well as many an able-bodied contemporary. Mickey Fingers' flying digits could tic-tac prices at incredible speed. Yardley was named after the scented bars because of his ability to soft-soap (flatter) his susceptible listeners. Sharing a taxi with him at the end of a race day at Glorious Goodwood, he claimed that it was only because of a forgotten toothbrush that he had had to turn down an invitation to spend the night in the house of the Duke of Richmond. Bloater's face would not have looked out of place on a fishmonger's slab. Peanuts was named after what he sold from a tray held by a cord around his neck. Porky's unkind critics felt his natural habitat should have been a pen. Lofty was just over 5ft, and Tiny was as tall as a Grenadier Guard.

Gambling was in the blood for all these men but, away from the racetracks and greyhound stadiums in the 1950s it was, of course, illegal. Nevertheless 'secret' gaming clubs abounded. How much effort the police made to stamp

Bernie the Bolt!

them out is debatable. Raids did take place, but underworld legend had it that many officers were prepared to turn the proverbial blind eye for a consideration. Apparently, a sliding scale existed; a half-crown for a sergeant and a shilling for a constable.

I once had to summon my father from Elbosses, our local den of iniquity. I managed a peep inside when the guarded door was slightly ajar. Billiard, snooker and card tables were just about visible through the most polluted atmosphere I was ever to encounter. The air was literally blue with the smoke of hundreds of Players, Senior Service and Woodbines, the latter being puffed by the less well off. The money changed hands frequently and noisily. How ironic it was that the money exchanged had travelled such a short distance from its origin – Elbosses was positioned just a few yards from the Royal

Mint. It is unlikely, however, that any person of eminence popped in for a few hands of Solo!

Eventually, my grandfather stepped down from his wooden stool and was replaced by my uncle Phil. George's retirement meant that I could become an active member of the firm as an apprentice who quickly mastered the techniques of clerking and the hand signals of the tic-tacs, to the obvious benefit of my pocket money.

The sign language of tic-tacking, by which price information was given and received and money moved around in betting exchanges, was employed at Clapton Greyhound Stadium as well as on southern racetracks. On night duty at the dogs, my hands were adorned with white linen gloves to provide a clearer visual impact. They bestowed on me a kinship with head waiters, magicians and safe-breakers. In the context of our modest standard of living, considerable sums of money were entrusted to me in this manner. I took the occupation seriously and was mortified if I made a mistake. I wanted to be known as having safe hands. This activity provided a kind of theatrical treat for first-time visitors. My fellow entertainers and I never drew applause, but I liked the idea of the onlookers believing you had some kind of mystical power not possessed by Mr Average. When errors occurred, the public's enjoyment was increased when universally known crude hand gestures were inserted in anger into the special language of the trade. Sometimes, before normal service was resumed, an instant sacking took place. These were the days before tribunals investigated unfair dismissals. I was lucky in that I was never sacked. Most of my jobs outside the family firm came from family connections. Nepotism rules OK!

One nice little earner involved the longest solo commute of my teenage life. My new boss was one of my father's uncles. For reasons I could never discover, Uncle Mickey had settled with his family in far away Reading, known to me from my train-spotting. It was an important junction; a gateway to the west. I had acquired further knowledge of the town through the geography O-level course as it featured in our study of the Thames Valley. The text book informed me that, within its bounds, (Huntley & Palmers) biscuits were manufactured and (Suttons) seeds packaged. The town also contained the famous gaol behind whose thick red brick walls Oscar Wilde had been detained for committing 'unnatural acts'. While inside, he penned a poem which was to give the building its significant place in English literature.

On Thursday and Saturday evenings for about a year, I travelled by the familiar Circle Line to Paddington station. From that great West London terminus, I then caught an unfamiliar main line train to my Berkshire destination. Mickey's elder son Henry provided a private taxi service.

I was picked up from the station forecourt and taken to the family's flat in a smart private apartment block. There I was wonderfully fed and watered by Aunt Rosie. Feeling satisfyingly replete, I would then be driven to Reading Greyhound Stadium where I operated as Uncle Mickey's clerk.

During my time there, the track provided a rare sporting incident – a three-way dead-heat. At the end of a closely contested race, the photo-finish camera situated on the illuminated winning line confirmed that the three little black noses of the leading greyhounds had arrived together. 'Sod's Law' dictated that it was the last race on the programme and three groups of punters had to share the winning pool. I was destined to miss my usual return train. Accordingly, it was past midnight when I arrived at Paddington, and the clock was approaching 1.00 a.m. as I took the first steps away from Aldgate station. There was more drama ahead. Middlesex Street, which led to our house, still contained some war-damaged buildings and bomb sites. As I passed what was left of a brick wall , I had an uneasy feeling that I was being followed. I had heard no footsteps and was aware of no human shadow falling across my path. My instinct was to bolt, but curiosity prevailed. I came to a slow and measured halt, and gingerly turned my head. Creeping silently along the line of bricks was an enormous rat. I then ran faster than any triple dead-heating Reading greyhound.

Uncle Mickey's family contained one other member. Cousin Roy was afflicted with Down's Syndrome although that term, named after the English doctor John Langdon Down's discovery in 1866, was little used in those days. As a child when first confronted with him at a family function, I was a little afraid and decidedly curious. I later asked my mother what was wrong with him. She stated bluntly and without embarrassment that he was a Mongol. The crude term was employed because such young people with that disability were thought to look like the inhabitants of a remote part of the Far East. Even harsher words were used but hopefully never before the person concerned and his protective parents. To my child's eyes, he seemed grotesque. His speech was often difficult to decipher. He would shout and then suddenly become quiet and maudlin for no apparent reason. He seemed like an infant in an adult's body. I felt uncomfortable in his presence and feared being touched by him. This posed a problem as he was very affectionate and tactile. At the same time, I tried desperately hard to conceal these feelings, but I doubt if I succeeded.

By the time Uncle Mickey was employing me, whatever maturity I had acquired improved the situation. It had also given me a colossal respect for my uncle and aunt. A dark rumour had circulated that, at Roy's birth, another uncle had tried to persuade a doctor to terminate his life but, whatever the truth of this, Mickey and Rosie would not have countenanced such an act. The love and care they bestowed on their younger son was tremendously moving. They cherished him as much as they would have an Oxbridge graduate destined for a Nobel Prize. The physical and emotional demands he made on them cannot be calculated. The most touching moments occurred when Roy said or did something that would have mortified the parents of a healthy child. They quietly corrected him with the most gentle of loving smiles. To my own discredit, I failed to inquire about Roy's predicament after Mickey and Rosie died.

# nine

# Robert

During my teenage years, therefore, I led a dual existence – racing man and schoolboy. My school the Robert Montefiore, simply know as 'Robert', was close to the Whitechapel Road, marked on the Monopoly board in modest, muddy brown. The school was named, I believe, after the first Jewish officer and member of the LCC to lose his life on the Western Front in 1915. This, strangely, was never pointed out to me during my stay. Like my primary school, it was a three-storey building, but larger – a destroyer rather than a frigate.

If I may have been unaware of its link to the First World War, I had unhappy knowledge of its connection with the Second. Opposite the school, across Valence Road, was what was left of Hughes Mansions. This group of tenements had had the misfortune to receive the last bomb dropped on London. I frequently stared across the playground through the wire fence. How ironic and tragic that those who perished should have died so close to the end of hostilities, having survived in such a vulnerable area for six long and dangerous years.

My form tutor for the duration was Jimmy Lloyd, a man of mixed French and Welsh blood. Jimmy was a stocky figure who wore a black beret and thin gold-rimmed spectacles. He wielded iron control. There is an element of the obsessive and blinkered in all teachers when it comes to thinking that their subject is the most important on the timetable, and Jimmy was a prime example of this mindset. I have no complaints for, due to his single-mindedness and industry, virtually the whole class acquired French 'O' level a year early. This may have constituted some sort of record in a state school at that time. To produce this result, extra-curricular tuition was required. Jimmy was generous with his time. He put in what are now called booster sessions. These constituted two hours on a midweek evening, which we were morally obliged to attend, and for which we did not pay him a penny. Nowadays, he might have been considered a sad case as he boasted that, in his bachelor state, he spent whole weekends marking. The class was carried along by the enthusiasm he had for his subject. We knew the words of the 'Marseillaise' better than 'God Save the Queen'; we could serenade visitors with Charles Trenet's songs and quote the fables of La Fontaine. He even produced an Anglo-French review for public performance.

Jimmy's obsessive nature spilled over into his great love of the theatre when the aforementioned show *Salad Days* hit the West End. Allegedly, he saw it eighty-seven times. Before I left the school, he generously presented me with two complimentary tickets and, with them, I made a date with my mother.

Jimmy's blinkered vision only deeply upset me on one occasion. It was a case of unfortunate timing. The soccer team was scheduled unusually to play an important cup tie during afternoon school. The P.E. department requested that members be released from their normal timetabled lessons. All the individual subject teachers agreed – except Jimmy. Inevitably I was the only boy earmarked for French at that time. His *'non'* was as adamant as General De Gaulle's later negative response to Britain's application to join the Common Market. I was devastated. Seeing the team and my replacement leave at lunchtime was like looking out of a window in Heartbreak Hotel.

The soccer saga was subsequently to deal me a far deadlier blow. Our team progressed to the final and I was restored to the team. The twist took a last disastrous turn when I scored the winning goal – for the other side. It was a classic misunderstanding between defender and goalkeeper, resulting in a spectacularly over-hit back-pass. Some compensation was gained with a league winner's medal. This achievement led to the distinction the following season of our school representing the entire district in a London-wide competition. We were to contest only one round against the prestigiously named Tottenham.

One of the most important sports lessons I received during my youth was the benefit of playing a fixture before a 'home' and extremely partisan crowd. Where a competition used a knock-out formula, a coin was tossed to decide who was to play at their favoured venue. On one such occasion, we lost the toss and were compelled to make the long journey north. The first half was played during school time on our rivals' playing field beside their school. No spectators were allowed. It was a tight contest and we scored what we hoped would be the decisive goal. At half time, the bell sounded the end of the school day. What appeared to be the entire population of the school then surrounded the pitch. The atmosphere became intimidating for the 'away' team. The crowd's bellicose and one-sided support seemed to add inches to our opponents' heights and 5mph to their leg speed. Conversely,

The 1959 football team with me kneeling beside the headteacher.

we went into our shells and ultimately conceded four goals. During those tortuous thirty-five minutes, we didn't even manage to enter the opposition's penalty area.

Horizons were further broadened when, in 1962, Jimmy organised a two-week trip to his beloved France. This was during the Algerian crisis and one wonders whether today's safety-minded educational administrators would have given it the go-ahead. The holiday had its memorable high and low points including the horror of our first acquaintance (in a *lycée*) with a toilet that was just a hole on the floor. There was also the walk through the Pigalle district in Paris accompanied by a Catholic member of staff, appropriately named Mr Pope. This pious man was approached by a pimp and asked if his preference was for a girl or a boy? I am still not sure if he understood the question.

On the Cote D'Azur, we stayed in a large private school. It was a hot August and the occupants of the boys' dormitory were warned against discarding pyjama bottoms, however uncomfortable they became during the night as there was a high risk of mosquito attacks. Inevitably, there was someone who knew better. As dawn broke, we were awakened by Jeffery Crego's screams. Through bleary eyes, we collectively viewed the hapless victim peering beneath his sheet. His horrified expression bore testimony to a Pearl Harbor-scale attack by the winged insects. An entire week in a Nice hospital was required to reduce his cricket ball-sized testicles to normal size.

During the week of Jeffery's enforced absence, a friend and I had an encounter with the United States Navy. We were only a little way off shore in a pedalo and were trying in vain to attract the attention of two attractive French girls breast-stroking in the clear blue water. Suddenly our focus was diverted. About a quarter of a mile further out to sea, well beyond the bathers, water cascaded from the emerging back of what appeared to be a giant sea monster which, when completely surfaced, turned out to be a submarine of the United States Mediterranean Fleet. Our curiosity was immense and, like other small craft in the vicinity, we approached the vessel. Clearly we weren't viewed as a security risk as no amplified voice told us to back off. Sailors appeared along the hull and set about a variety of tasks and officers peered over the rim of the conning tower. As we closed to within thirty yards of the boat, one of the sailors looked up from his work and asked us if we were French. We replied in the negative, and admitted to being English. At that moment, a large wave carried us unexpectedly and quickly close to the ship. The pedalo swivelled and gave the submarine a sideways nudge. Luckily no damage was caused, and our new-found ally shouted in mock outrage, 'Hey fellas, are you trying to ram us? I thought you limeys were supposed to be on our side!'

Back on shore, we sat at an outdoor café table trying to impress our mates with what had become the equivalent of a fisherman's tale. Being thirsty, I ordered my first coffee in France. To my intense disappointment, a miniscule cup appeared containing a thick black liquid. When the time came to settle the bill, the waiter demanded the equivalent of half a day's wages of an assistant street vendor. My astonishment nearly outweighed the earlier sighting of JFK's warship!

International relations took another turn when, during our journey home, we stopped overnight at a *lycée* in Grenoble. We shared the canteen with a group of German students. This was my first ever close contact with 'the Master Race'. There was no communication between the two groups of visitors but the peace was disturbed by the evidently angry entrance of a young man who joined the other Germans. On his face was a look of furious incredulity. 'He wants to invade Poland again,' I commented to my friends jokingly, not understanding a word of what he said. The shouted words were also overheard by Jimmy who was later able to offer a translation of '*Sie wird nicht mit mir schlafen*' (she will not sleep with me). Germany frustrated again!

The major speculation about Jimmy was his sexual predilection. Today, his seemingly inseparable relationship with a few rare blonde boys in the school would have led to an official probe. We simply smirked or shrugged bemused shoulders and neither the girls nor we were in the least bit bothered by his blatant favouritism. I don't believe that any open disapproval would have bothered him as he allegedly possessed physical as well as moral courage. Rumour had it that he served in the French Resistance and had a number of narrow escapes from the Gestapo. Whatever the truth of it all, I owe him a big *'merci'*.

Jimmy's status as an outstanding teacher did not go unchallenged. In 1960, a handsome stick-thin Indian arrived to teach history – Manabadrula Mitra. This was the man my uneducated self had been waiting for as he added political colour to the study of the subject and laced its telling with rampant atheism. From him, we gathered that he had experienced long periods of hunger in the sub-continent and that he scorned religious taboos. Manab and his German wife had an 'open' marriage. When I informed my parents of this last disclosure, my naïve father believed this to mean that, when the couple went on holiday, they left their key with the neighbours. A natural charmer, Manab was certainly ready for the coming sexual revolution.

His popularity soared when he declared an interest in horse racing and unashamedly entered the newly opened betting shop on his way to and from school. When I tipped him a winner, he presented me with a ten shilling note and suggested I take my girlfriend to the pictures. He added mischievously that the seats in the back row provided the most entertainment.

He chain-smoked through lessons, holding the cigarettes in an inimitable style between nicotine-stained fingers. He claimed that all the headmaster's best ideas were his and that the transformation of the school was largely his doing. He was the first to tell me that universities were not just places on maps. He and Jimmy were barely on speaking terms. I would have loved to have been a fly on the staff room wall when they had a verbal set-to. Out of Manabadrula's earshot Jimmy referred to him scornfully as 'Napoleon'.

In my book, another candidate for the best teacher was Mike Jones. He came from Swindon and taught English and P.E. with a West Country accent. His trench-coated figure would check our names outside the train station for the weekly excursion to the playing fields of Fairlop. He led by example and joined in the matches with wonderful enthusiasm although, sadly, little skill. He volunteered to take 'the toughs' for reading and writing, and scandalised Jimmy by disposing of suggested texts and supplying comics, probably purchased out of his own pocket. The students had a whale of a time with 'Jonah'. Someone informed me that he later became a High Court Judge. I rest my case.

Dr Rhodes Boyson was the Lancastrian headmaster whom Manab claimed he advised. This highly energised and ambitious person was the school's publicly acknowledged reformer. He later became a national political figure,

Sixth form prefects with (Sir) Rhodes Boyson (clasped hands on left) and Jimmy Lloyd, standing right. I am standing next to him.

easily distinguishable with his grey Gladstonian side-whiskers. When he entered Margaret Thatcher's government as the Parliamentary Under-Secretary at the Department of Education and Science in 1979, he became a recognisable face on television and later received a knighthood. My mother became an ardent admirer of his and, when she moved to his Brent constituency, faithfully gave him her vote. Rhodes Boyson succeeded in expanding our horizons. In the summer of 1963 he organised an outward-bound experience for us deprived inner-city kids. The location was in his own beloved north-west. Our hostel was Hammerbank, a large country house on the shore of one of Britain's great lakes. It was allegedly the home of one of Queen Victoria's Prime Ministers, Sir Robert Peel who earlier in his political career, as Home Secretary, had founded the Metropolitan Police force. This gave those of us who lived near Liverpool Street a passing connection with the historic event for, above the entrance to its police station, under the blue lamp, stood a 2ft model of a 'peeler'.

The area of outstanding natural beauty near the hostel contrasted dramatically with our own home environment. From our climbs to the various summits, the view presented was as far as the eye could see. On our streets, the next corner was often the limit of our vision.

The day we left was to become an infamous day in modern history as it broke with news of the Great Train Robbery. The carriages that carried us back to Euston actually crossed the section of line near Leighton Buzzard where the mail train had met its fate on the previous night. We naturally rubber-necked from the windows to see at first-hand the massive police presence. From this local spot, an investigation would follow a trail that was to lead to Ronnie Biggs in Brazil.

In total contrast to Rhodes Boyson, his deputy Mr Rees was the most modest and lovable of men, but he presented a frightening exterior because of an acute squint. When he pointed at a miscreant and shouted, 'You, boy!' the eyes seemed to focus on someone yards away. The resulting confusion would lead to his greater outrage, and more merriment for those not directly involved. His travel to and from school seemed incredible to me as he lived in the distant Haywards Heath. I felt this put him in the same league as Captain Scott.

Dusty Miller taught woodwork. He became part of school legend for once approaching a boy planing in a lack-lustre fashion, and telling the idler to get some elbow grease into the task. The naïve pupil asked him where he could find some. Dusty hid his smirk and instructed the boy to go forth and seek. The lad did this for some time to the huge amusement of both staff and pupils.

Mr Arter – inevitably nicknamed 'the Farter' – was a curiosity. Few teachers in the area had a car but he drove a Bentley. Some said he had private means and owned several businesses. Why did he ever teach at our school? Was this a geographer who had taken the wrong path?

It was in Boyson's newly created sixth form that I first developed an interest in writing. Always aware of the value of publicity, our ambitious head proposed that the school should launch a newspaper. If it were produced by the pupils themselves, even greater kudos could be gained.

I had already been honoured with the title Head Boy. For everyday purposes, I displayed a small metallic shield on the lapel of my blazer. On ceremonial occasions, a royal blue ribbon, worn around my neck, supported a glistening and rather embarrassingly large medal. In view of my status, I was asked to edit the as-yet unnamed publication. My hesitation in accepting the job was understandable. Added to a total lack of experience were the demands of three A-levels and the possibility of university entrance. The time-consuming nature of my existing extra-curricular activities was another consideration. To undertake another demanding and unknown role could tip the balance adversely from possible success to certain failure in my little world. On the other hand, the sound of the word 'Editor' appealed to me, as did the thought of my name appearing on the front page. Ego triumphed over caution and I took on the job of running the perhaps predictably entitled *Sixth Sense*.

Only three editions were produced in the year. I wrote most of the articles but had to find a finer mind to compile the not-very-demanding crosswords. A local sweet shop proprietor, I suspect as much out of pity as of self-interest, agreed to advertise for someone to help me.

In that pre-computerised age, an enormous amount of my time was spent on compositing to ensure that the words appeared in neat columns as in a proper daily paper. It became something of an obsession and the nights before publication often saw me working well into the small hours. Mindful of American films that featured overworked reporters, I fancifully considered the idea of buying and wearing a visor. When certain of being alone, I could not resist a little extension of the drama and practised exclaiming, 'Hold the front page!'

The cold douche of reality brought me down to earth. My schoolmates did not form lengthy queues when the publications eventually rolled off the presses and sales could at best be described as modest. My mother actually bought a substantial percentage of each issue! In the last edition, I became a very low-key drama critic. The English department produced *The Wizard of Oz* and, as it constituted a major school event , I was duty bound to cover it. The partisan audience, largely consisting of doting parents, lapped it up. They were enchanted by the story, the characters and the melodious score. In fairness, justice was done to the juicy leading roles by the performers. Dorothy was endearing and her rendition of 'Over the Rainbow' brought tears to many a sentimental eye. The brainless Scarecrow, cumbersome Tin Man and the cowardly Lion amused everyone with their quips and antics. The art department took full advantage of the colourful nature of the show as the Yellow Brick Road and Emerald City brightened up the normally dull hall. The costumes and make-up added spectacularly, and sometimes hilariously, to the riot of colour. Dorothy's real name was Sandra and the Lion's was Richard. I still wince a little at my chosen headline, 'Richard wins his Lion Heart and Sandra the Garlands!'

This amateur foray into journalism did, however, cause me to reconsider the newspapers read by my family. I decided that the household's *Daily Express*, though still of interest, did not stretch me enough. I decided to spend part of my racecourse earnings on extending my knowledge and widening my vocabulary. Possibly for the first time in its history, our local newsagent was requested to order the recently founded *Sunday Telegraph* and the older *Observer* (a bow to the Right and the Left!).

Boyson was a ball of energy; a man of action. He was a bit eccentric but whether this was studied or natural was open to debate. He had examined the great military leaders of the past and had learned that success could be sometimes achieved by the most unorthodox of methods. When old and trusted strategies failed, it was time to think 'outside the box'. I like to think that he had the Nelson touch; an apposite distinction given his naval background. This ability was linked with a roguish, even childlike, sense of fun. The school corridors would often be filled with the sound of his broad Lancastrian accent and his great guffaws of laughter – usually the result of his own impish jokes. Robert was far from being a place of educational excellence when he came aboard. The ship's company contained many a rough and tough diamond, a host of likely lads in need of correction. This was, after all, the age of the Teddy Boy, soon to be followed by the Mods and Rockers. Boyson's Five-Year Plan required a disciplined base. The dissidents had to be tackled – they had to be removed or improved.

The key contest between the new headmaster and the more disruptive of the students was the flagrant cigarette-smoking in defiance of school rules. At every break and lunchtime, smoke would rise from behind the walls of the senior boys' lavatory on the far side of the playground. Pupils had got away with it for years, consistently flaunting all admonitions and warnings. Their early warning system, a series of bribed or intimidated juniors acting as look-outs, proved completely effective. At the first sighting of an approaching member of staff, dog ends were flushed down toilet bowls or chucked over the external wall. The miscreants were never caught in the act, their nicotine-stained fingers a status symbol among fifteen-year-old leavers eager to join the outside world of adulthood.

From his lofty captain's chair on an upper deck, Boyson gave the matter much thought. Nobody aboard the ship was going to get the better of the skipper. An idea worthy of the victor of Trafalgar struck him and C.S. Forester's legendary Hornblower would have been similarly delighted with his ingenious solution. After a few minutes of a morning break with the mutinous smokers heading for their usual pitch, Boyson rang the local fire brigade. His emergency call informed them that the outside boys' toilet at Robert Montefiore School appeared to be on the verge of a conflagration. Within minutes, the Whitechapel Road was reverberating to the clamour of fire engine bells. The entire student body was brought to a fever pitch of excitement, their pleasure being enhanced by the knowledge that there was no real threat to life.

Boyson, masterminding the situation, was positioned at the school gate dramatically directing the crews to their objective. Within seconds, the well-trained men were hosing great arcs of cold water over the walls of the 'burning' building. The sight of the emerging soaked and spluttering former puffers staggering out into the fresher and much drier air became the stuff of legend. They could have no cause for complaint, they had been beaten at their own game, they had been hoist by their own petard.

Like the victims of Evelyn Waugh's incorrigible Brigadier Ben Ritchie-Hook, they had been biffed by Boyson. England should have expected nothing less!

# ten

# *The Brady Bunch*

Free of school in the evening and weekends and post my Bar Mitzvah, I was permitted to join the Brady Club.* This had been founded at the turn of the twentieth century and was supported by the LCC and donations from moneyed and generous Jewish benefactors. The Barnett-Janners, eminent representatives of the legal profession, were two that I can recall. There were others, many of whom preferred to retain their anonymity.

The leaders, referred to as managers, were volunteers. Some were ex-members who had risen from the ranks but the majority were outsiders with middle-class accents. Their commitment was total. They organised activities, trained and selected sports teams, and planned and accompanied us on holidays. They supervised the table tennis and snooker tables, and officiated at matches. When necessary, they provided timely and diplomatic interventions when disputes seemed on the verge of spilling over into fisticuffs. If coaches were full or unavailable, they transported us in their own private vehicles.

During my years with the club, its dominating figure was Yogi Mayer. He was a tall, muscular, thick-accented German Jew who had escaped from the Nazis and then fought courageously against them in a special unit of the British Army. Yogi was adored as a man and loathed as a referee. When teams were informed that he was to be 'the man in black', a cry of anguish could be heard. So scrupulously upright was he that he seemed to bend over backwards in favouring the opposition. We felt that no end of injustices were perpetrated on the altar of his integrity.

---

* Brady was a leading light of the ethnic association of Jewish Youth Clubs and a member of a broader national organisation.

The venue for most of our club football matches was the famed Hackney Marshes. This massive grassed area contained around a hundred pitches. They were a delight for boys whose normal kick-around took place largely on unforgiving concrete outside their flats and houses, traffic permitting. When the swirling autumnal mists descended, bringing visibility down to less than five yards, it could become an intimidating place. On a number of occasions, individual players and even entire teams got disorientated and then lost. If these confused wayfarers came across the frame of a goalpost, the numbers printed on the cross bar often provided the sole clue for navigation. When conditions eased and a match eventually got under way, the most apt piece of sports reporting might have referred to an outside right 'ghosting' down the wing.

In the summer of 1957, I was chosen from the junior section to join the advance party at the club's summer camp at Bembridge on the Isle of Wight. Although this was considered a great honour, it was to be an interlude I did not enjoy. The seniors made me feel superfluous to requirements and behaved in a patronising manner. I resented their little insider jokes and lingo. On the first night, I curled up in my camp bed clearly unhappy with my surroundings and obviously homesick. Yogi forsook his manifold tasks as commander-in-chief and took time to squat by my side. He stressed the impending arrival of my own age group and the exciting activities that were planned on our behalf. I'm convinced he then had discreet words with my fellow pioneers for the next day there was a marked change in their manner.

As promised, the day dawned when my friends alighted from their coach and I undertook my responsibilities as captain of the canvas. Inter-tent competitions got underway, as did the excursions to the nearest beach. We day-tripped to Sandown. There I triumphed at pitch and putt and sampled cream doughnuts.

Maurice Silverman's parents came down in a hired car. I was privileged to be their touring companion in the Baby Austin. We ventured to Ventnor and on to Freshwater Bay and The Needles. There in a kiosk that displayed all the brightly coloured paraphernalia of a seaside holiday, I purchased the inevitable glass lighthouse with coloured sands. This miraculously survived the remainder of the camp and the coach and train journeys home.

Night manoeuvres, far below commando standard, were greatly enjoyed. Afterwards, mugs of deliciously sweet glutinous piping-hot cocoa were served to 'the troops'.

During one particular day exercise, Yogi went beyond the bounds of his own bag of military surprises. As the attackers approached the enemy headquarters, a two-seater, open cockpit, single engine aircraft flew overhead. From the rear

A Brady Bunch team on Hackney Marshes. I am first left on the front row.

seat, a goggled and helmeted Yogi released water-filled balloon bombs. No missile hit its target but the bombardier sportingly gave a thumbs-up sign as the plane banked away. We couldn't wait to return home and inform those who had not attended the camp of Yogi's version of the Dambusters.

There were certain daily camp rituals. One that we all relished took place in the main marquee where we were fed and watered. It was inaugurated by the mass chanting of the theme tune from the BBC Radio's *Sports Report*. There then followed the reading of the latest sports results by a manager from his morning newspaper to the accompaniment of cheers or groans.

The other ritual was not so enthusiastically greeted. This was 'prayers' by the flagpole at the top of which the Union Jack loyally fluttered. A square was formed with the boys on three sides and the managers left and right of the flag. One fateful morning, our stunned ears heard a crack and splintering at the base of the white woodwork. Everyone froze as three quarters of the mast fell earthwards. The look on the face of the unfortunate manager at the moment the object landed on his head was indescribable. His knees buckled and his body crumpled to the ground. Fortunately his recovery was amazingly quick but the freak accident, like Yogi's aerobatics, became the stuff of club legend.

That camp also brought me to notice Barry Lissner, a highly talented cricketer. Barry was unusual among my friends as he came from what was then not common – a single parent family. His mother brought up Barry and his sister with the help of her parents. The grandparents were local characters. Grandmother was universally known as 'Bessie Toffee Apples' because she sold them from her stall in Petticoat Lane. Visits to Barry's home delighted the nostrils and before crossing the threshold, you could smell the sweet sticky substance being cooked. There, in the midst of fumes or fog, lingered the smell of distant orchards. Even though it might wreak havoc with our teeth, we couldn't resist the satisfaction of biting into the crunchy, hard fruit.

Ben, Barry's grandfather, was present on my first trip abroad to Belgium in 1960. The other first was taking to the air. A prop engine plane rattled its way up the runway of Southend Airport so noisily I thought its various component parts would drop off as it left the ground. Fortunately, it remained in one piece as we flew over the Channel and we landed, shaken *and* stirred, at Ostend. It was contact with the element of fire rather than air that led to the main problem on that holiday. Courtesy of Ben and his chain-smoking in bed, we were evicted from three hotels which refused to contemplate further damage to their linen. Only the presence of mind of those dispensing room service and the strategic placing of extinguishers prevented major conflagrations.

Barry's natural flair for cricket made him the first choice when skippers tossed for players in street cricket. I had always resented this but only at that camp did my bruised ego finally acknowledge that he was the better man with the bat. To his gifted eye, the little red cork must have appeared to possess the dimensions of a football as he stroked and clattered it all over the makeshift ground.

Due to the intervention of Lenny Carton, a rotund figure who sported the 'bacon and eggs' tie of the Marylebone Cricket Club, Barry was granted and passed a trial at Lord's, quite an achievement for a boy born closer to Eton Manor than Eton College. Sadly the family could not raise the money required to enable a professional, and maybe even an international career, to develop. I have often mused that Barry might well have achieved world recognition as a Test cricketer had there been a greater demand for toffee apples.

It seems strange that an East End boys' club had a country house but Brady did. Another rich benefactor had bought and donated Skeet, a rambling detached house with extensive grounds. It was situated near Orpington in Kent.

Two cameos remain. The first involved a Sunday morning cross-country treasure hunt. One question threw an interesting light on the upbringings of people from different cultures. I was in a group led by a non-Jewish manager from a local grammar school. He was amazed when the easiest question, in his opinion, received a blank response. 'A place frequented on Sunday mornings'. We thought the answer must lie beyond the immediate area we were in. The quizmaster had inserted a tricky one with a home link. Our responses therefore included Petticoat Lane and Hackney Marshes. The surprised manager then informed an equally dumbfounded group that the correct and obvious answer was the grey Gothic edifice in front of them – the parish church.

Although I was one of the first Brady Boys to go to university, I was far from the brightest. Joel Salkin was cursed with an overweight body but blessed with an overweight brain. His father 'Schpruntzy Lou', labelled so because of his sartorial elegance, may not have been the easiest man to get on with. A family row led to young Joel venturing to Skeet unofficially when it was closed. There, in the library, he spent time reading Dickens. When the news broke, the non-literary among us wondered what the 'dickens' he was doing! The slightly more knowledgeable took in the information with a sense of wonder and Joel's status as the boy genius grew. Years later, he appeared successfully on a TV game show where his extensive general knowledge was appreciated on a much wider scale.

Michael Morris was another Brady Boy. His youthful self-confidence more than compensated for his lack of inches. His dedicated following of fashion added to the likelihood that he would one day sample the sweet smell of success. Even when injured, he was mindful of his appearance as well as his comfort. At one summer sports practice he arrived in a pair of ultra (one of Michael's favourite 'mod' words) smart slippers. The purpose of the footwear was to protect some bruised toes. One wit remarked, out of Michael's hearing, that he might have been more at home in a hairnet than a cricket net.

Michael was, however, to have the last laugh on the subject of style. Many years later I was watching the TV programme *This is Your Life* as, on that particular night, it had a horse racing theme. The life being celebrated was that of the ebullient and popular jockey Frankie Dettori. As the proceedings were drawing to a close, the presenter referred to Frankie's eventual retirement from the saddle, and his far-sightedness at exploring different career opportunities. He mentioned, for example, that he had already made an impression as a male model. The live audience and millions of viewers were now to be introduced to the next guest who was described as a leading figure in the world of global fashion. This person, now a close companion, had assisted Frankie in the initial stages of the venture. The camera panned to the top of the steps at the rear of the studio stage, the music swelled and a beaming Michael Morris descended to greet his only slightly shorter friend.

In my late teens, the sports managers believed that, in addition to developing some cricketing skills, I was showing leadership qualities. On reaching the senior section of the club, I was awarded not only the captaincy of its team but that of the entire association of Jewish Youth Clubs for the London area. Only one match was played – a Jewish version of Patricians versus Plebeians. Our opponents were from Carmel College, the only Jewish public school, I believe, in England, which was situated in leafy Berkshire.

A coach picked up the team as it threaded its way westwards out of London. My father, a rare spectator at one of my fixtures, had a foreboding that the day would not be ours when the vehicle broke down several times. It coughed and spluttered its way along the A4, through Slough (which I then regarded as a very upmarket town) and beyond. Eventually it passed through impressive wrought iron gates and negotiated the long drive to the main school buildings.

My peg in the changing room was beside that of Barry Lissner whose name would have been the first the selectors wrote down. The coin was spun on an immaculately kept wicket; I lost the toss. We were to field against the best equipped and best dressed team I'd ever seen. Their cricket, however, was not as good as their immaculate kit. Strategically successful field placings and efficient bowling saw their innings conclude far below a hundred.

One of our openers departed early and Barry at number 3 instigated a speedy demolition of their attack. It was then that the opposition's captain and teaching staff, feeling that God was not paying sufficient attention, ordered the match to stop so that prayers could be said. Our amazement turned to anger but our protests were to no avail. Despite the blast of our outrage, the rabbis stood much firmer than the walls of Jericho. The day, which was intended to bridge the gap between the haves and the have-nots, almost ended in a class war. The match was drawn as a result of divine intervention.

A few years earlier, a personage far higher than the rank of rabbi visited the club. To commemorate the opening of some new premises which included a gymnasium, the Duke of Edinburgh himself agreed to do what he allegedly liked doing best of all in life – cutting the red tape. I was one of hundreds seated cross-legged on the floor of this sports hall as the duke carried out his inspection. As he strode by with hands clasped behind his back in the familiar pose, I was struck by the crease in his trousers and the shine on his shoes. The event made a big impact locally. Most of the members of my family were thrilled by the visit and spoke of the inhabitants of Buckingham Palace in tones of awe. My communist cousins, however, disassociated themselves from what they regarded as sentimental and dangerous clap-trap. They reminded me of what had been the fate of the Tsar of all the Russias. Fortunately assassination was not on that night's agenda. Had it been, the only missiles available were ping-pong balls.

Alongside the Brady Boys' Club was its female counterpart and fraternisation was encouraged by the mid-week social. On the parquet floor of the communal hall I took my first steps at the jive. This we danced to the sounds of Elvis, the Everly Brothers and Buddy Holly from the States, with Cliff and Co. providing the home-grown version of rock 'n' roll. Managers of both sexes moved around the edge of the proceedings, trying to hide inane grins. There was no violence, however; only during the slow numbers did any sort of physical activity take place.

The pressure to follow a 'fashion fad' was intense. Your dance floor credibility could be ruined if you wore the wrong shreds or shoes. Greasy rockers were despised and mods were the gods. The male of the species disported himself in tight-fitting, box-shaped jackets of Italian design supplemented by clean white collars and slim ties. Adam Faith's head for some time provided a template for the desired hairstyle, although Brady didn't have many with fair hair. Winklepickers with attached Cuban heels had their moment. They could be purchased in a variety of leathers, with crocodile skin enjoying a wide popularity. I wonder how many orthopaedic surgeons now owe rich pickings to ancient feet permanently deformed by those who favoured this fashion in footwear?

Success on the dance floor could result in couples pairing up. Amorous anticipation soared when one of our groups (usually a girl) was permitted to have what was euphemistically described as 'an evening in'. These were petting parties when optimists hoped they might do more than pet. With parents absent, the opportunity presented itself for the boys to see how far they could get and for the girls to decide what, despite their mothers' warnings, they would permit. Dancing took place in the living room. As the evening developed, couples would move off to any bedroom or recess available. The temperature rose and clothes later had to be readjusted but it's difficult to quantify how many lost their virginity.

At one such gathering, my principal loss was my dignity. I had cajoled one of the girls into a vacant bedroom. Soon after reaching the horizontal, disaster struck. Just when I imagined I was about to take off into another stratosphere of sexual activity, a most violent cramping attacked the back of my left leg. My loud exclamations were of agony, not ecstasy. This was a sexual encounter that left me limp in a totally undesired way.

My mother, perhaps like many of her generation, exhibited double standards when it came to sex and her offspring. She would not have objected (may even have derived some satisfaction) if I had been acknowledged as the local handsome Romeo with a flock of admirers, many of whom I had deflowered. On the other hand, my sister was instructed to always ensure that her particular branch of the Underground remained firmly closed until her wedding day. My father never mentioned the subject and I forgot to tell him the facts of life.

My father's naïvety and embarrassment about sex never failed to amuse and sometimes astonish the family. Bernie Levine and, perhaps surprisingly, my mother related the two most telling anecdotes.

During the late 1950s and early '60s the 'Jolly Joe' and 'Webb' firms combined forces, but probably not a lot of cash, for a business trip to the famous May meeting at Chester races. Enormous crowds held out the prospect of rich pickings. The cost of a Manchester boarding house, where Monty and Bernie probably shared a bed in Eric and Ernie mode, would hopefully be covered. After an unusually successful day by their standards, Bernie decided that they should go on the town and visit a nightclub. My gullible father assumed this to be a place of entertainment, but the two northern 'comedians' had in fact mischievously booked a table in a striptease joint. To add to my father's further embarrassment they were to occupy a front table. When the principal 'dancer' appeared wearing only a G-string and a tasselled bra, restraining hands had to be placed on my father's shoulders. These weren't to prevent him from pouncing on the girl, but from leaving the premises. He then received the stripper's personal attention. One assumes her pretty palm had been greased beforehand by the devilish duo. The swinging tassels closed in on my father's terrified eyes. The culminating piece of choreography was the not unimpressive skill of landing a tassel in his pineapple juice. The girl then returned to the upright and suggested that my father suck dry the dripping material. Apparently his face drained of colour and he appeared on the verge of passing out. At that point, Bernie later confessed, he thought the joke had gone too far. Fortunately, my father's self-control asserted itself and the show continued. My father left without his parched lips touching the glass containing his overpriced fruit juice.

The second encounter of a sexual nature occurred in my mother's presence on the other side of the Atlantic. My sister Bernice emigrated to the States in 1975. Two years later, my parents made their one and only visit. My cousin Sandra had preceded my sister in settling in New York and, during my parents' holiday, they were invited to their niece's Manhattan apartment. Sandra was a liberated lady and had never been short of male company. At the time of my parents' arrival she had recently chosen a partner in marriage. The routine of matrimony had not, however, restricted her sexual imagination. Mother and father were hospitably offered refreshments and, before departure, given a full tour of the extensive accommodation. The highlight was the de luxe master bedroom. On the ceiling above the queen-sized bed was a full-length mirror. This article was to become the focus of the story that became a family legend. My father observed the mirror first in perplexity and then in annoyance, but refrained from making any judgement or comment out of respect for his gracious hosts. When he and mother were safely ensconced in their own modest hotel room, he expressed his confusion and anger. Why hadn't his niece demanded action and compensation? The stupid workman should be forced to remove the offending mirror from the ceiling, and reposition it in its proper place on a wall.

# eleven

# The Siegies

Despite the shared love of horse racing with my father, I felt a closer bond with the maternal side of my family. My mother Nancy was the ninth of eleven children – her mother was born Rebecca Delmonte and claimed to be related to the bearers of the same name that appears on tins of peaches.

An even more exotic connection is said to exist via the latter to a barely credible fisherman's tale. In the 1930s, the *East London Advertiser* published a photograph of my mother's clan with the caption 'Princes and Princesses of Labrador'. Thus ran the story behind the headline. An alleged ancestor was one Samuel de la Penna, a seventeenth-century Dutch fisherman. During a particularly rough day at sea, while in charge of a vessel, he went to the aid of another in obvious distress. One of the first-class passengers was William of Orange. Later to be King of England, the Dutch Master was then in control of the Netherlands themselves, plus a newly acquired empire. On safely reaching terra firma the grateful celebrity expressed his gratitude with a gift of incredible magnitude. He announced that he was bequeathing to Samuel and his descendants the Province of Labrador. Though a largely barren and often breezy place, not the most clement of habitats, it still constituted an enormous chunk of real estate. I have often wondered whether William was trying out his English and actually meant to present his lifesaver with a dog.

The story was picked up by the local weekly paper when the case between the family (in its very broadest sense) and the Canadian Government over right of possession went before the Judicial Committee of the Privy Council in the House of Lords – the Canadians had no wish to be left without an Atlantic coastline. The judges decided in Canada's favour, and there ended the possibility of my being descended from 'royalty'.

The would-be king, my mother's father, was Louis Siegenberg. His large family, known as the 'Siegies', required enormous efforts on his part to sustain them at a time when state assistance was not as forthcoming as it is today. It is alleged that he often worked from 4.00 a.m. until 1.00 a.m. the following day. He had a variety of jobs; they might start at the dock gates and conclude in a billiard hall where he chalked queues and set up the coloured balls for the nocturnal players. How he found time and energy to procreate is a mystery. One of his daughters claimed that he only had to take his trousers off for Rebecca to find herself in the family way. The extent of his breeding was typical of the poor of the period. Whether those with the least means should have the biggest families was a contentious issue then, and remains so today all over the world. Selfishly, as the son of a ninth child, I'm glad Rebecca accommodated Louis so many times.

Had she been an Italian mama during Il Duce's dictatorship, her reward would doubtless have been a matronly medal of honour. Though far from unusual, her fecundity gave her a kind of local fame. At the end of her life, the renowned 'baby factory' produced what was to become a much quoted remark on her death-bed. She was to succumb to her last illness at the age of seventy in 1951. As she lay dying, an ambulance was summoned to 4 Herbert House. This vehicle inevitably aroused the interest of prying neighbours. At every level of the building, at windows and over balconies, people were gathering and speculating what was going on. As my grandmother was carried out on a stretcher by two sombre-faced bearers, a respectable hush fell on the air. Aware of the universal curiosity which she must have largely resented, she raised her head and her voice in order to reach the most distant ears. With one of her last breaths, she was determined to nip all rumour in the bud. 'Believe what you like, but I'm not bloody well pregnant!'

In the aftermath, my aunts and uncles were to pay tribute to their departed mother in a manner of which her jocular spirit would have been proud. Life, not death, was celebrated at a riotous level. My family's conduct was unusual set against the normal definition of a Jewish *Shiva* where the bereaved sit on low stools for an official reception of family and friends who offer condolences. The traditional atmosphere is one of respect and piety where the guests wish the mourners 'Long Life' and the prayer for the dead is recited. In Rebecca's case, in total contrast, the 'grief stricken' survivors, led by Uncle Joe mercilessly pulled each others legs about life-long foibles and indiscretions, sang ribald songs and told innumerable jokes. This seemingly inappropriate behaviour may have outraged the mildly religious and certainly the orthodox. The happy noise, however, drew the attention of those in the neighbourhood on the look-out for a good time. So great was the drawing power of the party that lengthy queues formed outside the ground-floor flat desperate to join the revellers.

Those who paid homage were extremely generous. To sweeten the sorrow, it is customary to bring cakes or biscuits. The guests were so grateful to be admitted that large numbers of expensive gateaux were delivered, and legend has it that their boxes were stacked up to the ceiling. At the end of proceedings they were shared among the mourners. A revealing postscript sheds light on how long sisterly rivalry and ill-feeling can last. A long-standing feud existed between the rough and ready Rachel and the snooty Dinah. Rachel assumed charge of the distribution of the cream cakes with the result that Dinah's share was only of the squashed variety.

Despite this light-hearted depiction of Rebecca's end, my mother grieved deeply for her for the rest of her life. If she had to convince a listener of the truth of a statement, she would add sincerely if somewhat oddly, 'On the life of my dead mother underground!'

# twelve

# Nancy

My mother Nancy was born at the exact minute of the murder of Archduke Franz Ferdinand, the incident that sparked off the First World War. If there is such a phenomenon as the transference of souls, do I have another tenuous link with a famous historical figure?

Although father was my great provider, whenever favourable racing results allowed, Nancy was my great supporter and staunchest defender in a crisis. She provided physical comfort in her fleshy arms when I was tormented by pain and words of solace and encouragement when I was emotionally down. Her calm presence allayed any fears I might have.

As a child, I was very frightened of the Big Bad Wolf of fairy tale. The long fanged jaws, the red eyes that burned like hot coals and the elongated claws regularly featured in my nightmares, and meant that I slept with a night light. Family members, who evidently thought I needed toughening up, would jest about a visitation from the hairy hound. My Auntie Rachel (Ray) and my Auntie Kitty went a step further on one never-to-be-forgotten occasion when they were staying in my grandmother's ground-floor flat. My customary sprint brought me to the door. As I raised my five-year-old hand to knock, the letter box flew open and out shot the inanimate claws of an imitation fox fur. This got the intended response. Hilarity was occasioned by my involuntary scream and jump of terror. Nancy was not amused and told the perpetrators to pick on someone their own size. This was a family phrase often used when some action smacked of bullying. Naturally the episode did the rounds of the relatives to my everlasting embarrassment.

The same pair teased me mercilessly about my first love. Soon after the brush with Basil I unwisely made it obvious that I was enamoured of Marion Lazar, an older woman aged seven. Whatever chance I had of a favourable response was ruined by the 'terrible twins'. Whenever Maid Marion appeared and I and they happened to be present, the air would be rent by raucous cries of 'Here's Marion, Jeffrey.' A furious blush lit up the beloved's face and I bolted to some safe retreat far from the mischief makers. I'm sure no real harm was intended and I subsequently became indebted to them when they sagely pointed out that more lasting love might be found with someone closer to my own age.

Ruth(ie) Joseph was the prettiest girl in my class. Never did I speak of my feelings, but they ran deep and proved that Marion mania was light-weight by comparison. Ruthie could have been the brown-eyed, gold-earringed, plait-haired doll placed in a gypsy caravan in a child's picture book. 'Tragedy' struck when her family moved to a council estate in Stepney, a full 2 miles away, causing her to change schools. On only one further occasion did I catch a glimpse of her. During a Jewish holiday, a number of teenage groups chose the Tower of London as a place to congregate. I believed that our eyes met, but she appeared to turn deliberately away. I was devastated and toyed momentarily with the notion of using the conveniently placed bridge and the dark cold water below it.

My mother was raven-haired and full-figured and, I felt, quite attractive. Why she never married until she reached thirty puzzled me. Was it a case of Henry the First? As a girl she had been a keen swimmer and diver, once accidentally hitting her head on the hard base of the pool. In the 1930s she also enjoyed the popular pastime of ice skating. In the 1950s and '60s she relished the black and white TV coverage of the figure skating competitions. I inherited no love of $H_2O$ either in its liquid or solid form. My skinny frame trembled even in heated indoor baths and only once (unsuccessfully) did I take to the glassy surface of a rink.

Mother was most at home in the kitchen. Her culinary skills crossed the cultural divide. She harboured a yearning to turn professional and claimed that she could have managed a deli or a café, supplying bagels or bacon with equal success. Father would not permit her to try, no wife of his needed to work. She loyally accepted his decision. Nancy's cuisine nevertheless kept my stomach supplied with a much-loved menu of speciality dishes. Matzos and lentil soups, chopped liver, gelfilte fish, kreplech, viennas and lockshen pudding constituted staple and much-appreciated ethnic fare. Roast beef and Yorkshire pudding, toad in the hole, bubble and squeak, fish and chips and Irish stew were among the highlights of the traditional British dishes she turned out.

My mother was as committed a shopper as she was a cook. She had a great rapport with the vendors of fruit and veg and with the poulterers and butchers in their noisy nooks. I enjoyed observing the trade at the many-coloured stalls, but flinched at the smell and touch of the dead flesh in the shops. Removing the innards from a fowl or stuffing a turkey at Christmas were two unbelievably heroic tasks that she performed.

Bargain-hunting took her beyond the bounds of the market on our doorstep. Wickhams was a departmental store, impressively housed in a domed building on the Mile End Road. Mother became addicted to this emporium, occasioning father to dub her, half in jest, half in exasperation, Mrs Wickhams.

My personal preference was to accompany her to Gardiners which stood in the triangular site at the junction of the Whitechapel and Commercial Roads. At this outfitters in 1952 my mother purchased my first football kit – a green and white quartered jersey with collar, white shorts and green and white hooped woollen socks. I'm uncertain as to why these particular colours were chosen, but their acquisition led to some kind of allegiance to the far-off Plymouth Argyle.

Occasionally, there would be ventures to the wonders of the West End. Gamages in Holborn was an essential stopping-off place on the outward journey. The toy department contained mouth-watering exhibits – two inch metal guardsmen in scarlet and black, small-scale Spitfires, Wellingtons and Lancasters, and a model railway layout that covered more floor space than our entire flat. Hamleys in Regent Street was a toy town in its own right. By the end of my childhood, a wicker basket was set aside to hold the remaining items of my parents' generosity. Sadly, it and the now-valuable miniature toys it contained have long gone.

In my late teenage years, there was a head-on clash with my mother regarding the ethnicity of my girlfriends. Her (not particularly pious) wish was that I would court and marry 'a nice Jewish girl', the celebration of which would be a full-scale traditional Jewish wedding with the added bonus that (unlike the Bar Mitzvah) father would not be footing the bill! In my early and middle teens, the issue hardly arose as school and the Brady Club were largely Jewish environments and the risk of association with other girls was minimal. Although uncomfortably aware of anti-Semitism and the proximity to the Holocaust, I could not accept my mother's inverted racism, even when acknowledging that it was in part a defence mechanism. I was equally appalled at a rabbi's suggestion that the presence of so many flowers at Christian funerals was to mask the smell. The insulting vocabulary of retaliatory prejudice caused me to wince more and more as I got older. English girls were referred to as *shiksas* or *tollers* and were only good for one thing! The boys were labelled *yoks*. For the generality of non-Jewish people the word *goyim* was employed.

It was only my cautious mention of dating on my return from university that ears pricked up and I could sense the tension. I admitted to having romantic relationships with a few female students. My mother saw and cut through the bland nature of the language with her sarcastic and accusatory comment, 'Don't they admit Jewish girls; I thought they were supposed to have brains!'

Both my marriages to non-Jewish women constituted massive betrayals and disappointment for her. Before each wedding, she supplied an embittered eleventh-hour comment, 'In the end you'll always be a mean Jew!' The harshness of the remark was the product of a genuine dread – perhaps understandable but hardly justifiable. For example, my wife Susan has the kindest of hearts. During our joint viewing of *Schindler's List*, she sobbed throughout much of the film and as the final credits rolled to the haunting soundtrack, the remnants of an entire box of Kleenex lay at her feet. Hers were not crocodile tears.

Perhaps surprisingly, my mother also had prejudices within the Jewish community. In the nature of the diaspora, Jews came from a number of European countries to settle in the East End. Both sides of my family came from Holland. Nancy described us as *cuuts*. The word was always enunciated with warmth and affection. We were a minority within a minority. The bulk of the immigrants were the descendants of those who had fled the pogroms in Eastern Europe, their former home being the Pale of Settlement in Poland and Russia. My mother referred to them contemptuously as *pullucks*. As far as she was concerned, they were beneath her in class and definitely not to be trusted. Had I married a girl from this demographic strain, her happiness would have been tinged with reservations. If a friendship of mine with a boy with such connections came to an acrimonious end, she would unhesitatingly comment, 'What can you expect; his lot give us good Jews a bad name!'

Her feelings, particularly when angry, ran deep. Even within the family, a dispute with a sister could lead to the most bitter of divisions. After one monumental row, she declared, 'I'll never talk to her as long as I live!' Happily, in the course of time, she relented and at her death was on speaking terms with them all. In her sweeter moments, she could be incredibly sociable, her proud boast being, 'Me? I can talk to anyone!' On trains, buses and planes, she would start up conversations with strangers (in spite of her underlying prejudices). This mortified my father who was an incredibly shy man outside his own comfort zone. 'Why do you keep talking to people you don't know?' would be a familiar and despairing plea. 'How can I get to know them if I don't start talking to them?' she would counter, and then castigate him with 'Look at you – wouldn't say boo to a goose!' My father never had the last word!

## thirteen

# First Born

The previously mentioned Auntie Ray was the first born of the Siegenbergs, emerging at the dawn of the last century in the midst of the Boer War. She was arguably the most comical of the cluster. Her biggest admirers would not have described her as a May Queen – more like a fading Mae West by the time of my acquaintance. Her make-up was not discreet; heavily rouged cheeks and crimson slashes of lipstick glowed like the top traffic light. Rumour had it that, as a girl, she sent herself Valentine cards and signed them from 'an unknown admirer'. She waited but didn't weight watch. Patience or perseverance were rewarded as she eventually lost her maiden certificate to Aaron Feld. This uncle was so Jewish-looking that he was ironically dubbed 'Spud'. Interestingly, he was closely related to the early 1970s rock star Marc Bolan.

A First World War veteran with battle scars on neck and posterior, Uncle Aaron was the most mild-mannered of men. At the table, he ate his food at an incredibly slow pace. This commendable example of manners may have been a hangover from the Western Front – when in khaki he may have believed that his current meal could well be his last. Despite this passive nature, however, two of his much-used personal effects fascinated and scared me. Around his waist he wore the broadest of leather belts with a massive buckle; an awful instrument of chastisement, it seemed to me, although it may never have been deployed for such a task. And, when shaving, he continued to use the open razor supplied to him as a soldier to the King.

On leaving his country's military service, the local council employed him as a rat catcher. I relished descriptions of his 'uniform' as he descended into the subterranean passages and areas below the tenement blocks. A balaclava and huge scarf provided his head and neck with protection and his cuffs and trouser bottoms were tied tight with cord. In one gloved hand was a fustian sack in which were deposited the dead rodents and, in the other, the heavy wooden club that put them there. Thus attired and equipped, he dared to face any carrier of unimaginable diseases he came across.

It was said that neither the rats nor the Kaiser's grey-clad gunners frightened him as much as one of Auntie Ray's tongue-lashings. These were often the product of Aaron's post-pub activities in the Feld household's toilet. For a military veteran, he had an appalling aim. After a night of downing double scotches in the Bell, he would ascend the fire-step on which his WC was mounted and fail to hit the bowl with monotonous and disastrous regularity. To compound his crimes, he often omitted to lift the seat. When it was Auntie Ray's turn, she became indecorously unbalanced by a slippery floor and then experienced the unpleasantness of depositing her rear on a wet platform. Neighbours assured the family that she did not suffer in silence.

Their joint exit from the 'local' was an event in itself. My sister and I would regularly be woken when the fat lady started to sing. We could not remain asleep when it seemed like a thousand 'goodnights', addressed to fellow drinkers, were chorused at maximum decibels, alongside ribald songs. Peering from our window in the small hours, my sister and I would witness the amusing antics of the respective constables of the Met and City forces. Rather than have the physical hassle and paperwork of dealing with drunks, the blue and white cuff bands would haul the bodies across the Middlesex Street border on to City territory. An hour later, those wearing the red and white cuffs would return the compliment – the policeman's version of Pass the Parcel.

Despite her lack of catwalk credibility, Auntie Ray clung steadfastly to the opinion that men found her charms irresistible. When a group of Asians moved into one of the neighbouring buildings, she was one of the first to extend the hand of friendship. Aaron quietly chuckled at her amorous advances towards Abdul and Said. She also established a rapport with the only black gentleman in our part of the ghetto. A very smart dresser with a white wife in one hand and a lead attached to two white dogs in the other, he aroused speculation as to how he made a living. Whether Auntie Ray was ever privy to this information is not known. Long odds were available if you wished to wager that he offered her a job.

Two other exotic characters inhabited Auntie Ray's little world of dubious glamour. Ivan the hairdresser and his inseparable friend Paddy were the two resident homosexuals. Ivan was a far cry from Fred the Barber on whose wooden plank, resting on the arms of his swivel chair, my hair was first cut. In an age before the ubiquitous splashing of deodorant, Ivan did not smell like other men. He sent forth an aroma not dissimilar to the scented air around my mother's dressing table. His distinctive mincing gait was one not often seen on the football pitches of Hackney Marshes. Nevertheless, in that politically incorrect age, he was accepted as part of the community and I hope was never the victim of 'queer-bashing'. He was always courteous and my mother always commented on his wry sense of humour. Paddy appeared more of an extrovert and he exuded a certain Gaelic charm. He and Ivan never forgot Auntie Ray's birthday or, rather quaintly, her and Spud's anniversary.

Like so many at the time, Auntie Ray was betting mad. In the days before betting shops, wagers were struck over the telephone (blower) with unofficial bookies willing to accommodate clients over horses or greyhounds. Auntie Ray never wished to be seen as a loser. She therefore irritated her fellow punters within the family by declaring, whenever the result of one of the big races was broadcast, that she had backed the winner. It appears that she wasn't lying in that she covered all the options by backing every one of the runners. This involved an inevitable small loss each time she gambled but it seems that she was happy to accept this in order to publicly claim victory.

Auntie Ray also stood out as a very effective employer of swear words. This had to be viewed against the back-drop of an area where profanities were common. Few used such words with as much natural fluency as she did, particularly when she suddenly tired of your company.

Her ailments were many and well publicised in family circles. She used a manifestly painful limp to win the sympathy vote when in need of allies. The image was augmented by her rolled-down surgical stocking, which for me never quite had the attraction of the nyloned glamour girls that adorned the pages of my mother's *Woman* or *Woman's Own*.

My aunts and my mother often fell out over outspoken differences of opinion or betrayals both real and imaginary. The rows could be short-lived little spats or more lengthy and bitter feuds. One would be informed that Aunt X was not talking to Aunt Y and that Aunt Z had treacherously sided with one or the other. My cousins and I were generally amused by these developments but occasionally embarrassed if our respective mothers fell out as alliances moved like shifting sands. The most significant clashes would occur over arrangements for Bar Mitzvahs, weddings and funerals. The offending party would have either attended or not attended the event, thus giving monumental offence.

Auntie Ray had a son. She named the infant Emmanuel at registration, but he was known as Manny within the family. My mother held him in high regard and accorded him with her most complimentary accolade – obliging. Twelve years my senior, he became one of my boyhood role models and was one of the cousins who encouraged mother to consider allowing me to attend a university. In addition, when I was eight, he urged me to support the

Lillywhites and took me to my first Spurs match against Middlesbrough who wore distinctive maroon shirts and included the England international Wilf Mannion in their team.

Manny played as well as watched football. Prior to watching him display his characteristic side-footing of the ball, I was allowed into the dressing room. There my nostrils first became acquainted with White Horse liniment and my eyes with jock straps. My immediate thought was concern about whether I would ever develop enough credentials to justify wearing such an appliance.

Manny, along with many of his generation, was 'called up' for National Service, in his case with the Royal Inniskilling Fusiliers. When he returned on his first leave in full rig topped by a feathered cap, he seemed like a hero.

The Korean War was making the headlines in the Felds' *News Chronicle* in 1950 and Manny was scheduled for an all expenses paid trip to the Far East courtesy of the British government. By this time, he was in love (and it lasted a lifetime) with Irene, an attractive brunette. Manny boasted that she was extremely posh as, unlike himself who spent his nights on a fold-up bed in the living room of his parents' flat, she had her own room. Coincidentally, 'Goodnight Irene', sung by both Frank Sinatra and Jo Stafford was one of the top numbers in the hit parade that year. Manny proceeded to play this minor classic interminably on a cranked-up gramophone with the sound issuing from its trumpet horn. Fortunately he continued only with 'goodnight' and not the anticipated 'goodbye' of leaving the country since he and a few of his contemporaries were ordered off the troop ship bound for Japan due to a technicality relating to qualification for service overseas. At that time, Manny was none too pleased to be released from his patriotic duty. However, the eleventh-hour reprieve restored Auntie Ray's faith in the Almighty since, in her opinion, her son had not taken a wrong 'Korea move'.

Auntie Ray's own wartime record contained a remarkable and inexplicable event. During the Blitz, she, Aaron and Manny occupied a first-floor flat in Brunswick Buildings. On hearing the air raid siren on one occasion, Ray had a quick though unnecessary tidy-up before prudently locking the front door. Her last domestic action was to kneel down and stroke the head of her beloved cat who was sitting quietly on the mat.

The Felds emerged from the shelter the next morning. At ground level they were gratified to find that, although part of the building had been destroyed, their section was still intact. On climbing the stairs and reaching their home, however, they were horrified to discover that the front door had vanished with no sign of what exactly had happened. Inside the flat, none of the furniture, ornaments or pictures on the walls had been disturbed in any way. The mat was still in place but the pet who she regarded as the best mouser in the district was never seen again. Like his namesake Lord Kitchener (this being Aaron's choice in memory of his service in the First World War) he had disappeared in mysterious circumstances. The key to the missing door was never thrown away but was found a permanent resting place in his Lordship's never-to-be-discarded milk bowl.

After the shock of losing her cat, Ray decided that her even more precious little boy should be removed briefly from danger and told her always-compliant husband that she and Manny were going to spend a weekend in Wales. It was to be two years before Aaron was reunited with his family! Ray did at times have an unpredictable streak although the separation was strangely amicable.

Aaron spent the time of his separation employed by a demolition company that specialised in cleaning up the tragic remains of bombed breweries and distilleries. He freely admitted that perks went with the job in the form of liquid assets and that, as a consequence, he slept each night in a blissful alcoholic haze on sister-in-law Betsy's sofa. The lounge that housed this makeshift bed ended the Second World War smelling like a public bar.

In the postwar world, Ray's wicked, indeed cruel, sense of humour was typified by her treatment of street singers. These poor wandering minstrels would burst into sentimental ballads ('Yiddisher Mama' was a predictable 'Housewife's Choice') below tenement block windows. As the act concluded, copper coins would be tossed down in appreciation or pity. It was a living of sorts. The singers had a set itinerary and their listeners would know when they were likely to turn up. Armed with this knowledge, the mischievous Ray would heat up coins in her frying pan. Concealing her oven gloves behind the window sill, she would throw down the heated coins to the innocent vocalists. She derived enormous sadistic satisfaction from hearing their involuntary cries and seeing their frantic blowing on blistered fingers. One wonders whether her victims ever sought and gained revenge on the witch for her brew.

## fourteen

# Uncle Joe

The second Siegenberg turned out to be a boy. He grew into my mysterious Uncle Joe. In his youth, he fell for an abandoned waif called Maggie to whom Rebecca had given a home in her already overcrowded abode. The girl wasn't Jewish, and all the gloomy predictions about the mixed marriage that eventually took place were to an extent borne out. The union was a tempestuous one in which Maggie was largely responsible for the discord. This was the family's interpretation anyway, and some might question its validity. Whenever my mother mouthed 'Maggie', her expression was one of disapproval.

In the mid-1950s, Uncle Joe became the licensee of the Duke of Wellington public house in Toynbee Street. To guard the premises and its occupants, he acquired an Alsatian called Major. This ferocious-looking dog seemed the reincarnation of the Big Bad Wolf of fiction and it held an equal sense of fear for me and, when in or near the pub, I gave it the widest of berths.

Uncle Joe was a round, bald-headed man who reminded me of Winston Churchill, whom he greatly admired and supported. He was the moneyed member of the family although the exact source of his wealth was never revealed to me when I questioned my mother, and she always looked uneasy if I persisted with the interrogation. Her secretive manner and loyalty were understandable for, wherever it came from, Joe spread it around the family. When my sister Bernice required a corrective eye operation, and Aunt Kitty a deposit on a modest semi, Joe provided the funding.

These riches were a factor in Joe changing his name and attempting to upgrade his social status. Mr Siegenberg disappeared to re-emerge as the anglicised Mr Stafford. He felt he had attained some kinship to 'high society' when he became a racehorse owner – a far cry from the street corner betting slips of his entry into the 'Sport of Kings'. On one memorable occasion, he brought the 'colours' up to our flat. I was allowed to play at being a jockey and, for five blissful minutes, put them on. In the black jersey with the gold sleeves and the red and white hooped cap, I rode Siren Light to an imagined victory on the arm of our sofa. The whole episode with the racehorse ended in tragedy when, during one of its races, the horse mistimed a fence, sending its rider crashing to the ground and to his death. This terrible experience probably ended Joe's venture into ownership.

Uncle Joe spared nobody with his barbed quips. On one occasion he singled me out, perhaps deservedly, for such a sally. Owing to financial and geographical reasons, I decided that no family members other than my parents should attend my first wedding. Joe heard of the exclusion and took umbrage. He telephoned ostensibly to offer congratulations and to assure me that a cheque was in the post. Being an expert in comic timing, he fractionally paused then added 'as instead of arranging a family celebration you are having a benefit.' Before putting the phone down, he sarcastically requested to be the first to be informed if I was to become a father!

His 'wit' extended to the emotive subject of death. When a friend's funeral came to an end, an elderly and extremely frail man was left standing next to Joe by the open grave. As the mourners were about to turn away, Joe looked at the grey and gaunt skeletal figure beside him and muttered 'If I were you I wouldn't bother leaving.'

Years later, reading a book on the London Underworld, its author provided an explanation of Joe's activities. He defined my uncle as a fixer, a broker of deals between criminals and the police. Joe's dubious fame on the edge and probably outside the law, however, was eclipsed in terms of the Sunday papers by his second son Dennis, with whom I don't think I ever exchanged a single word. He allegedly became a juvenile delinquent due partly to the trauma of his evacuation during the war and partly to an education in crime provided by, of all people, his mother. Maggie appears to have been a female Fagin, actively encouraging her younger son to thieve by day and night. The most outlandish example of robbery involved equipping Dennis with a rubber dinghy. This float and its paddles enabled him single-handedly to board and plunder Thames barges as they lay moored at night. One pictures Dennis preparing for such illicit expeditions by blackening his face and hands in commando style. Perhaps as he scaled the sides of his targets a sheaf knife was held between his bared teeth. Morality aside, it must have taken a lot of pluck to tackle wind, tide and patrolling police boats in wartime. He must have risked not only drowning but being shot. What treasure he stole found its way to the infamous 'Black Market'. Did the recipients receive the stolen goods in a package marked by a skull and crossbones?

Dennis's wedding and guests with Uncle Joe to the right of the groom. Some of the attendees were members of the police force.

A future film maker wishing to portray Dennis's early life might entitle his production *The Pirate of Canary Wharf*. But maybe there is no need of such a film as Dennis later claimed that *Get Carter* was based on his exploits.

Dennis derided conventional and tedious ways of earning a living. Lacking neither ambition nor courage he went on to challenge the notorious Kray brothers – and lived!

His 'business' enterprises did not meet with the complete approval of the law enforcement agencies and he was soon a guest of Her Majesty. During an unofficial early departure from a place of correction, and while on the run with the police of many counties searching for him, Dennis apparently approached an officer and cheekily asked him the time. My mother claimed he actually went a provocative step further and informed the member of the constabulary that he probably didn't realise how near he was to promotion.

Incarcerated again, his notoriety became nationwide when he left Dartmoor in mid-winter without the governor's permission. Surviving a night of sub-zero temperatures by cuddling a sheep, so the story goes, he managed to exit the country. The long arm of the law eventually grabbed him in the much friendlier climate of the Caribbean where he had assumed another identity and acquired a healthy suntan. The popular press rightly regarded him as good copy. Dennis was the classic good-looking playboy who oozed charm and never wanted for female companionship. I possess a small photograph of his marriage to a glamorous model flanked by an array of smiling plain-clothes men who seemed to bear him no ill will.

Released some years later, he did not enjoy the rarefied air of freedom for very long. Operating in the Newcastle area providing entertainment establishments with one-armed bandit machines, he became embroiled in a gangland dispute. A shooting took place and Dennis was subsequently arrested for being at the trigger end of the fire-arm. He returned once again to what he may well have regarded as his natural habitat. His professions of innocence led to Uncle Joe submitting a succession of appeals and petitions to the authorities, culminating with the House of Lords and Downing Street. After many years, Dennis was released as a result of these appeals and headed for the southern hemisphere.

In 2002, Dennis was the lead item on TV news bulletins when he appealed to the European Court alleging infringement of his human rights. A gaunt-faced image made the front page of *The Times*.

## fifteen

# Overs Cast

Third in the Siegenberg line of battle was my Aunt Clara who became Mrs Overs on marrying my Uncle Mike. They occupied Flat No. 4, Herbert House, situated the other side of the infamous dust chute. It was their three sons Dickie (Richard), Louis and Davy (David) who were to greatly influence my formative years. They attempted to indoctrinate me with political and anti-religious opinions, encouraged me to study, and even take up golf.

Aunt Clara was the tallest of my aunts and the most authoritative. She had a very forceful personality. A volunteer for community service, she rather enjoyed the little bits of power that accompanied it. She was like Madame Defarge in *A Tale of Two Cities*, never happier than when telling people where to go and what to do. A surviving photograph catches her standing proud in her Red Cross uniform with her first aid bag over her shoulder. She had a bee in her beret regarding posture, barked instructions at her class during PT, and at me if I failed to stand straight and walk tall.

Her dictatorial, though without question well-meaning, manner even manifested itself in the kitchen. I needed no urging to eat the golden brown chips that were lifted from her frying pan but had to summon every ounce of courage to eat a raw onion which she insisted was the most effective cure for acne. I elected to face a near-death experience rather than openly defy her.

Uncle Mike was her consort battleship. Fractionally shorter and twelve years older he could have been accused of baby snatching, had not the term been totally inappropriate for Clara. Well into his sixties, he continued to work as a porter in Spitalfields fruit and vegetable market. His muscular body had no trouble pushing his barrow home at the end of days lifting and carrying not insignificant weights. On summer evenings, his handcart parked outside the flat provided my friends and I with a marvellously large toy. It

Five Overs to go – from left to right are Dickie, Davy, Aunt Clara, Uncle Mike and Louis.

became an improvised see-saw or, with a flight of imagination, a covered wagon or a fort.

Like Clara, Mike was a health and fitness fanatic, although he spoiled this somewhat by smoking. The latter involved the use of a unique cigarette holder – a filtered chicken bone which he handled with the aplomb of Noel Coward (who used one of slightly superior quality). However, I doubt whether the great aesthete cleared his chest and throat by spectacular projections of phlegm. These hit the yard if Mike was sitting outside his front door, or a spittoon if beside his fireplace. He was never known to miss.

Mike feared neither man nor God. Like Aaron, one of 'Kitchener's Million', he returned from the war with a greater contempt for his upper class officers (those who led from behind) than for the enemy. With his highly-developed working-class consciousness, he helped to organise the Porters' Trade Union and was inordinately proud to hold the first membership card it issued.

He was a supporter of the British Communist Party and an avid reader of the *Daily Worker*, supplementing his knowledge by the regular purchase of *Soviet Weekly*. His excitement knew no bounds when he learned how many thousands of tractors were coming off the production lines behind the Iron

Curtain. He was one of the few members of the family to turn the pages of the newspaper other than for the racing news.

He loathed rabbis and priests. When he considered me old enough, I was shown copies of the *Freethinker* and told of the great Charles Bradlaugh, the Victorian atheist who established the right of non-believing MPs to affirm their patriotic allegiance rather than take an oath on the Bible.

Mike was a rough diamond who was determined to bring me up the hard way. He had no patience or tolerance for any display of weakness. At Larkswood open air pool, his first swimming lesson was to throw me in at the deep end. I was, however, to have the last laugh on this most macho of men. In early teenage years, I inadvertently eavesdropped on Clara informing my mother with a mixture of jollity and disappointment that her sex life was virtually over. At sixty-two, Mike, in order to keep it up, would need a barrage balloon.

During the early part of the Second World War, the three boys were evacuated from the East End to East Anglia. It was decided by the authorities that Dickie would be separated from his brothers, a decision which did not augur well. Davy was the next to suffer from hurt feelings, experiencing an unusual example of anti-Semitism once his identity became known to his hostess. This woman already had preconceptions about the demonic nature of our tribe. She began carrying out an inspection of Davy's head. At first he wasn't troubled, assuming that the lady was carrying out a regulation search for nits. As her fingers parted his hair, he volunteered that the school nurse had already given him a clean bill of health. 'I'm not looking for lice,' she said, and added without a trace of embarrassment or apology, 'I'm searching for horns!'

Dickie was to avenge himself on another tormentor, a bullying farmer, by pouring weed killer on his cherished strawberry patch. Clara was subsequently to receive a series of pleading letters akin to distress signals. She then, like a protecting Hereward the Wake, waded into the Fenland and removed her flock from further victimisation.

Dickie was the eldest of their sons. He never had a proper job but I'm not sure that he actually wanted one. To his artistic credit, he did find employment as a professional actor, although his paid engagements were interspersed with long periods of resting. The closest he came to stardom was the not insignificant part of the Swiss policeman (bandaged and crutched) in the 1960s film *Zulu*. On his return from filming in South Africa, we were privileged to view some of the 'stills' before the movie went on general release. I was fascinated by the whole enterprise and amazed when Dickie disclosed that he was paid £400 for six weeks' work.

A few years later, I pressed him for more details about what had become a cult movie. He revealed that in the foyer of London's Prince of Wales

Theatre, he and Michael Caine were awaiting the summons of the casting director for their auditions. Allegedly, Dickie's then relatively unknown acting acquaintance expressed uncertainty as to how to read for the star role of Lieutenant Bromhead. Dickie suggested he should adopt the voice of 'an effete English aristocrat', and added that the interpretation should be 'burlesqued'. As far as I know, Caine heeded this advice. Dickie also maintained that he suggested to the producer and co-star Stanley Baker that he 'look no further in filling the role.' The rest is history.

Dickie's final link with the film was not as happy as the introductory one. He and Stanley Baker had a considerable difference of opinion and my cousin's contract was terminated and he was forced to leave the set. His task was then to return to the UK. Rather than spend his not inconsiderable earnings on the costly air fare, he chose to return by cheaper and less luxurious means. He travelled overland to Durban where he joined a merchant ship and worked his passage as a humble cook. Such are the ups and downs of show business.

Previous roles included the dubious distinction of portraying the mummy in *The Mummy's Shroud*, and the coach driver in *The Larkins*. During the shooting of the latter, Dickie related that the comedienne Peggy Mount who played Ma, informed him that she was the oldest virgin in the business.

Sadly for Dickie, Rorke's Drift was a watershed. After the cinematic re-enactment, Dickie's career went one way and Michael Caine's another. Despite this disappointment, he retained an interest in matters thespian. In a cross-family link he tried to persuade my father's youngest sister Rosie to give her daughter Sandra the chance to go on stage. My talented female cousin, the daughter of a Canadian soldier (Mo from Toronto), was denied the chance. Dickie had been impressed by her performance in the leading role of a school production of *Rose and the Ring* and felt she was a natural. His pleadings were in vain and my father's family even resorted to ridicule, referring to him as 'Professor Higgins'.

Perhaps because of their father's strongly held political opinions, all three Overs scorned the 'Establishment'. Dickie, for example, boasted that, when asked by the military conscription board to what religion he adhered, he replied 'What are you short of?' It is doubtful whether his irreverent rejoinder endeared him to the authorities.

It was not unusual for Dickie to be financially embarrassed. There were two indicators of penury. The first was the need to reside at Clara's flat and the second was the part-time job of acting as babysitter for my sister and me when my parents had a night out at the pictures. At 6ft 4in tall and in his thirties, Dickie was an unlikely aspirant to such a role. His height had always made him a marked man and he was inevitably accorded a nickname – 'Longboat'.

*Zulu* – Dickie 'saves' the star!

I relatively recently came across an illuminating reference to Dickie in David McGillivray's column 'Now You Know' in the June 1988 edition of the fondly remembered magazine, *Films and Filming*. He wrote, 'As for Dickie Owen, who as far as this column is concerned is a veritable Lord Lucan, I can only assume that he has a network of friends feverishly protecting his anonymity.'

Dickie had already converted 'Overs' to 'Owen' for stage and screen purposes. Family members who were aware of his cash flow problems thought it a particularly apt name. 'Dickie Owen – never pays'. Cynics might conclude that the search alluded to in *Films and Filming* was not in the cause of cinematic art but for debt collection.

The only other professional actor I can claim a very distant relationship with is Frank Rozelaar-Green. I was completely unaware of this man's existence (and he mine) until the 1990s. One morning, a colleague asked me if I had viewed a Channel 4 programme about Frankenstein, adding that the actor portraying the main role included Rozelaar in his name. I was immediately struck by the coincidence. Dickie had played the Mummy and Frank Frankenstein – two monsters. It did not say much for the family's looks. Despite this sobering fact, Dickie did in some way have the last laugh. When *Zulu* won widespread acclaim, he featured prominently in the action shot selected by the *Daily Mirror* for its centrefold. He may not have made page 3, but for the family he would always be a pin-up.

Louis was both the sophisticate and the handyman of the brothers. Like most of my older cousins, he would have been quite capable of entering higher education had he been born at a later date. He attended West End theatres as well as depositing his cab's passengers at their steps. He listened to classical music and at one point dated a student at the Guildhall. Prior to this, the only people we knew there were the cleaners. No do-it-yourself task defeated him and his deft hands could effect endless mends and repairs. His construction of a balsa wood jet fighter was a testimony to his skill at model-making.

Louis took up golf along with his younger brother Davy and they instructed me in the swing of a club, using the doormat of their council flat as a practice tee. The lessons moved on to the use of air-flow balls, accompanied by the cry of 'fore' to warn those descending the nearby stairwell of impending danger. I helped them repaint battered golf balls which were left out to dry on a little wooden bed of nails that Louis had constructed. They looked like the resting place of a dwarf fakir.

Louis was one of the first in the family to acquire a private vehicle. It was in this blue Transit van that I accompanied him to my first golf course – Whitewebbs at Enfield. Initially, I was understandably employed as a caddie where I was allowed a few surreptitious shots on far and uninhabited parts of the course. Only in my middle teens was I deemed sufficiently competent to justify the payment of a green fee.

One day while humping Louis's clubs, I received an insight into his sexual activities. The weather turning suddenly warm, he discarded his jacket. Rather than have an awkward 'carry', I decided to wear the oversized garment. Casually putting my hand in one of its pockets, I felt and heard the rustle of a small paper wrapper and removed it, hoping for a sweet. To my surprise, it was a 'packet of three'. Quickly replacing the article, I spent the remainder of the round speculating about Louis's prowess with a different set of balls.

Louis certainly took the game seriously. Although not as big a hitter as Davy, he was uncannily accurate with the chipper and the putter. This led to him achieving the distinction of one year making the last eight of the *London Evening News* amateur matchplay championship. At the start of the competition there had been a huge field so his progress to the quarter-final was no mean feat. His explanation for his defeat at that stage was that it was due to a sartorial misjudgement on his part. He had decided, unwisely as it turned out, to wear on a beautiful summer's day a smart canary-yellow shirt. His hope was that his physical appearance would tilt the psychological balance in his favour. He could not have made a worse judgement. The chosen shirt may or may not have impressed the human eye, but it certainly drew the attention of hundreds of flying insects which pestered him for eighteen irritating and extremely uncomfortable holes. His game fell away with each bite and, in consequence, the match was lost and, with it, the chance of lifting a much-coveted trophy. Understandably, Louis took a jaundiced view of the day's proceedings. The offending garment with its speckled array of dead gnats was never seen again. Thereby layeth the sting.

The Overs were eager to praise but also had no reluctance to criticise if they believed I had overstepped the mark in any way. Their favourite word in this context was 'leery'. My little group of friends often became the Seventh Cavalry and I was accorded the imposing and inaccurate rank of general by my troopers. The Overs dished out some verbal stick if they heard my pretentious title being used in the play areas. I once committed a most dishonourable act in a rare clash with my sister. The throwing of a squashed peach was unfortunately witnessed by Louis who instantly ordered 'Big Boy Bollowallah' to report to him. My friends fled, and I was crestfallen to receive a smack around the head.

I did, however, prove useful to my two cousins in acting as their prompter when they learned 'The Knowledge'. This refers to the examination administered by the Carriage Office of the Metropolitan Police to ensure that officially credited taxi drivers know their way around the maze of London's streets. Each day, an aspiring cabbie would cycle or motorcycle with the charted routes on a clipboard attached to the front of his two-wheeler. In the evenings, I would often hold the script while Louis and Davy recited the streets, with all their left and right turns, between any two given points. Periodically they would present themselves at Scotland Yard to be tested. If the examiner approved of their rate of progress, they would be recalled at closer and closer intervals until the great day arrived when they would receive the badge. A man's success depended on his own powers of memory and the amount of time he was prepared to put into the task. Louis was a high flyer and won approval in six months. It was alleged, however, that my first love's father was eventually and only granted his license to sit at the wheel of a black cab on a vote of sympathy.

A coincidence associated with this episode involves the chief examiner. The cousins and their colleagues fervently prayed, before a test, that they would not be greeted by examiner Finlay. He was a crusty Scot with a beady eye, imperious manner and an impenetrable accent. By chance, his son Ian has been a teaching colleague and tennis companion for a number of years.

If prepared to put in long hours, the bachelor cabbie cousins amassed considerable funds, enabling them to leave our cold shores during the 'kipper season', the period between New Year and March when trade annually slumped. In the late 1950s, they would regularly take a midwinter break in the Canary Islands, then an almost unknown and unvisited part of the globe. When they spoke of Tenerife and Lanzarote, they might just as well have been talking about a place on the moon. They always hoped to pick up not just a suntan but a bit of Spanish.

Louis's professional driving was interrupted by an unfortunate and embarrassing episode. Chancing his luck, he ventured into a nice little earner with his cab that regrettably backfired. This was permitting his public vehicle to be privatised by prostitutes and their patrons, resulting in him losing his licence on the grounds of immorality and constituting a hazard to road safety. The magistrates took a dim view of his scheme to provide thrills on wheels. A red-carded Louis decided to extend his travelling arrangements and spend some time in the USA. A family photograph captures a night when he phoned home. In the 1950s, trans-Atlantic calls required advance booking, so we all dutifully assembled at 4 Herbert House. I can't recall whether I was one of the privileged few to hold the receiver and talk long-distance, but we all shared in the general euphoria occasioned by a wonder of modern science.

My debt to Louis extended to his advocacy of my university application. He, like Manny as mentioned before, encouraged my mother to stand up to the protestations of my least favourite Uncle Phil. The latter on first hearing of the suggestion exclaimed contemptuously, 'What's he going to be – a f***ing doctor?' Fittingly, it was Louis's taxi (the licence regained) that conveyed me and my suitcase to King's Cross station in October 1963 to catch the train for York.

The last and the youngest of the Overs family, Davy, was perhaps the one with whom my association was to be the longest. He and Louis generously bought me my first golf bag and half set of clubs for my thirteenth birthday. Dickie may have made a contribution, but it probably only sufficed to cover the cost of a tee. Davy was the family's outstanding sportsman. Both he and Louis lifted weights to enhance their 6ft-plus frames. I looked on in admiration at their bulging biceps and contrasted them mournfully with my own stick-thin arms.

In the early 1950s, Davy took part in a professional boxing bout as a heavyweight. I was a member of the raucous crowd that witnessed the contest, and have vivid memories of the night. The air was dense with smoke. The spectators were in shadow in the vast hall but, in its centre, the ring was brilliantly lit. Davy wore silky blue shorts with a white stripe and the emblem of a Star of David. A cut above Davy's eye ended the contest with the referee's verdict being a technical knockout. The bell that terminated proceedings also ended Davy's short-lived career with padded gloves.

As a boy, Davy had been selected for Westminster schools at cricket. My only opportunity of seeing him play was when Dickie involved us in an actors' match one afternoon in Regent's Park. Davy produced a stylish innings several classes above those who were clearly much happier treading the boards than the wicket. Davy was accomplished on water as well as on land. His collection of trophies was a tangible tribute to his accomplishments in the pool and from the high board.

Soon after taking up golf, he broke into the prestigious single figure category and represented Mocatra, the taxi drivers' society. On his return from an international across the border, I listened in awe to descriptions of the depth of the bunkers and the size of the greens at St Andrews where the match was played. He must have cut a dashing figure, in the heather or on the fairway, in the tam o'shanter which he wore in honour of his appearance at the home of golf. Even today, approaching eighty, his handicap remains in single figures and his enthusiasm is unabated. If he is on the golf course or at the driving range and unable to answer his telephone personally, his recorded voice informs the caller that he is out, not practising his swing but perfecting it!

Davy's desire for perfection laced with style once manifested itself during his days as a smoker. He took a fancy to the cigarette holder but, unlike his father's primitive hollowed-out chicken bone, he purchased a modern and sanitised piece of equipment from the shop of a superior West End tobacconist. In the 1950s and '60s, even non-smokers could experience an aesthetic pleasure when entering such premises. Gleaming racks of pipes, bulbous jars of leaf tobacco and exotic labels on packets of foreign cigarettes assaulted the eye, and the mixed aromas invaded the nostrils. When I became an occasional smoker, my own favourite brand was to be the exotically named 'Passing Cloud'.

A jingling bell greeted one on entry, and the smiling proprietor or assistant was always courteous and informative. You felt Dickens would have felt at home there. Like many a convert, Davy's zeal for the new-found love increased and he became dissatisfied with his initial relatively modest-sized holder. His sixth and final buy measured no less than 9 inches. With a glowing cigarette attached, it almost constituted a weapon.

Late one glorious summer morning Davy and his appendage were sheltering from the sun under a shop awning in Piccadilly. He was sporting a new suit with a matching tie. In his own words, he 'looked the business'. After a few posed puffs he happened to turn his head west in the direction of Hyde Park Corner. Strolling along the pavement towards him was an even more elegantly dressed man. The latter's lapel was adorned with a buttonhole consisting of a bright red rose. It was not, however, the flower that established Davy as second best in elegance. Unbelievably, his 'rival' was holding between his fingers a foot-long cigarette holder. As the range closed to ten yards, Davy made another discovery. The Gent had a gap-toothed grin and one the most famous and recognisable faces of the time. It was that of the great English comedian, prankster, film and TV star Terry-Thomas.

The game was on. David stepped out into the path of not Goliath but T-T. The two pairs of eyes locked, but the challenges held twinkles, not sneers. The ready wit of both appreciated the moment, but it was to be a *High Noon* of comedy, not tragedy. To the amazement and delight of watching pedestrians, they simultaneously shouted 'En Garde!' and adopted the fencers' starting position. They then crossed and clicked cigarette holders and, for one hilarious minute, fought a mock duel. A lucky witness claimed it rivalled the great and hugely popular swashbuckling efforts of the then silver screen – Fairbanks and Flynn would have raised their masks and blades in admiration. The only risk to life from Davy and Terry's efforts would have been if a member of the non-paying audience had died of laughter. The dramatic climax was achieved when the two warring cigarettes fell at the same time from their holders. Each 'swordsman' stamped on the other's glowing ember. *Touché!*

Davy's sporting life was at one time blighted by his mother. He bitterly resented Clara's insistence that he forsook playing football for Brady in order to assist her on her Petticoat Lane shoe stall on Sundays. Many years later I had the misfortune of being present during a slanging match between mother and son when this episode was dragged up. The recriminations showed that many of childhood's emotional scars never heal.

Like his father and brothers, Davy believed in this life and not in the next. You could feel him squirming above shuffling feet when required by family duty to attend religious ceremonies. Always a background figure on these occasions, you could sense his stony silence when the congregation was called for a response.

Like Manny and Louis, he encouraged my academic ambitions but claimed that history could only be studied from a Marxist base. When he presented me with the Communist Manifesto, it was done with a reverence Rabbi Newman accorded the Old Testament. I actually thought with my boyish naivety that it was a cracking read. 'Workers of the world unite. You have nothing to lose but your chains'. 'Capitalism carries within itself the seeds of its own destruction.' 'Religion is the opiate of the people.' These ringing phrases slipped into my mind as easily as the oil into the engines of Uncle Mike's beloved Soviet tractors.

The Overs linked the theatre with politics and, on several occasions in the early 1960s, this led to me joining the duffle-coated, ban-the-bomb audiences at the Unity Theatre in Camden. My cousins' intention slightly miscarried for it aroused my interest in old time music hall rather than the left-wing intellectual offerings of Brendan Behan and Bertolt Brecht. At that theatre, Dickie had made several contributions as a scriptwriter. He prided himself on a parody of Pinter's *The Caretaker*, entitled *The Pintaker*. The thought that the future Nobel Prize winner might have heard about Dickie's mickey-taking is mercifully unlikely as one suspects that his dark humour would not have found it funny.

The Overs were the only punctiliously clean family that never bathed in their own home. Their bathroom functioned as a mini warehouse for Clara's stock of shoes, the bath itself overflowed with ladies', gents' and children's footwear of all shapes and sizes. Unfortunately my mother never had the moral courage to buy Clarke's instead of Clara's with the result that I have hammer toes on the end of my feet. It was another way in which visits to Number 4 could prove 'sole-destroying'.

The Overs used the public baths in nearby Goulston Street. When requiring something more than a simple bath, they would go the extra mile to Ironmonger Row. There, in a volcanic atmosphere which I never had the courage to enter, they indulged in Turkish bathing. The conclusion of this activity required a plunge into what must have felt like ice-cold water. This form of torture was said to open and close the pores.

The Goulston Street washhouse had, during the Second World War, provided a hugely embarrassing moment for many and a simultaneously comic one for a few. A V1 rocket landed close to the building during its daytime use. The peculiar nature of the resulting blast did not destroy it in its entirety but just removed the street-facing wall. There were no casualties but it is difficult to gauge how much mental anguish was inflicted on the rudely exposed bathers. Never in the field of human bathing was so much showed by so many to so few!

The philosophy of bodily worship extended beyond its life span. Uncle Mike was determined that his body should be of value to humanity after his demise. When the family was informed that he had donated it for the advance of medical science, Auntie Ray was scornful. She declared that his 'orchestra stalls', if sent to a jeweller, could be turned into a pretty set of earrings.

In the tough school of hygiene the Overs, however, had the last word. The conclusion for a sedentary visit to their WC necessitated the use of what can only be described as sandpaper. There was the rub. Overs and out!

Not that many had the last laugh on Mike or Clara. My ten-year-old friends and I persisted in kicking a football against the walls and around the yard of Herbert House. The incessant banging resulted in the fraying of the nerves of the older inhabitants, particularly those living on the ground floor. To our discredit, we were callously indifferent to their pleas to go and play somewhere else. We even defied Clara, whose door and kitchen window were beside the infamous dust chute door which was employed as one of the goals. She stormed out when one particularly hard shot rang against the metal and threatened murder if we did not clear off. An outfield player gave her a cheeky response and she rushed back into her house, slamming the door. The next incident was to cause her anger to boil over. A misdirected shot broke the glass of her kitchen window when she was standing at her sink. The offending object and the fragments of glass ended up on the potato peelings. Clara emerged again from the house at high speed, brandishing a kitchen knife of frightening proportions in one hand and the ball in another. The bang of the perforated ball punctured the air and was followed by a manic hacking and ripping of the deflated rubber. She flung the remains at our stunned feet. Any man who crossed Clara was lucky to leave with his balls intact.

# sixteen

# Great Scotts

unty Betsy caused a mini sensation in the late 1920s when she married Arthur Scott. This uncle, in order to win her and placate the family, had changed his religion and undergone circumcision. He went on to be one of the most popular of avuncular figures and was described as 'a true English gentleman' by many who had harboured initial reservations.

In the mid-'50s, he had a very serious illness. The suddenness and life-threatening nature of the attack shocked us all, and the degree of genuine concern manifested throughout the family indicated a deep sense of attachment. He happily survived, but remained an invalid for his remaining years. I recall him as a sedentary man with a disproportionately sized stomach which I suspect was connected with his illness. Whenever one saw him in his flat, he would have an enormous mug of tea close to hand. Betsy's beverage always had to be served hot and sweet.

Uncle Arthur was a supporter of West Ham United and accordingly gained much pleasure from England's 1966 World Cup triumph. The legendary Bobby Moore was captain of both England and the Hammers, and two of his Upton Park team-mates, Geoff Hurst and Martin Peters, also played significant parts in the achievement of the national side. Even the Spurs and Arsenal fans in the family were delighted that Uncle Arthur lived to see that great July day.

My aunt had two addictions – smoking and betting. There was no cough in the family to rival hers. Giving up was never a serious option and she could have inhaled and puffed for England. Our front door was often opened before she had time to knock for the constant hack warned of her approach.

Betsy's betting rivalled Ray's, and I can recall the former's mouth twitching with self-righteous cynicism at some of the latter's more outlandish claims of success with the bookies. Their gambling, when it got out of hand, caused the immediate relatives a lot of anxiety, concern naturally centring on the debts they feared their respective mother or wife was accumulating without their knowledge or approval. Rumours circulated about the rows and rifts caused by these financial dealings.

Their two sons, Arnold and Louis, were likeable, humorous and intelligent young men who were not, however, as close to me as Manny and the Overs. Both did National Service in the RAF. In addition, Arnold displayed his academic ability when he became fluent in Spanish after studying at evening classes. This will have helped his successful courtship of Maria Carmen.

Louis had the distinction of being the first cousin to marry and the first to divorce. He had been a gifted footballer. Liverpool offered him a trial, and West Ham gave him a place in their 'A' team. I was hugely impressed as a ten-year-old when, on entering Betsy's kitchen one day, a quartered claret and blue shirt with crossed hammers and a number in bold white lettering could be seen hanging on a clothes line. In 2008, a letter from Liverpool FC was read aloud at his funeral. The speaker was a representative of the Humanist Society who conducted the service. It was the first of its kind that I had attended, held in a respectfully filled crematorium chapel in Colchester. Louis had a lovely, gentle sense of humour accompanied by a boyish chuckle which he retained as an old man. As his coffin slid forward through the silent, closing curtain the mourners heard Louis Armstrong's distinctive voice through the sound system. The Louis being honoured had selected the rousing 'Oh, when the saints go marching in' as his final serenade. A lightness of heart was felt, and I had to exercise self-control to prevent my feet involuntarily tapping to the beat. As the great jazz singer's voice faded, my neighbour in the row, cousin Larry Siegenberg, surreptitiously gave me a nudge with his elbow and quietly quipped, 'Beam me up Scottie!' If the deceased was able to hear the remark, I hope he saw the funny side from 'the other side'. Who knows?

It was the Scott family, and particularly Uncle Arthur, that my sister Bernice was drawn to. Nancy gave birth to her my sister in 1950. Prior to the event, I recall being rather embarrassed by the all too obvious bump in her stomach when I was dragged around the lane on a shopping expedition. Everyone else seemed in a congratulatory mood and completely unaware of my discomfiture. My feelings were probably the subconscious product of sibling rivalry. I had certainly enjoyed the notion of being the only apple in my mother's brown eyes.

Despite the close confinement of the flat where Bernice and I shared a bedroom, the age and gender difference kept us largely apart. The incident of the thrown peach aside, there were few clashes. I could perhaps have been a bit more protective but I was uncertain how to handle the kid sister relationship in front of my contemporaries. I was certainly pleased for her when the National Health spectacles she was compelled to wear from a very early age were no longer required. As mentioned before, Uncle Joe's money and the surgeon's skill removed the irregularity that could have led to the wagging of wicked little tongues in the playground.

As with me, my sister was to disappoint our mother for many years in the marriage market. Fortunately for her, Bernice and I do not look remotely alike and my mother was often quizzed by mischievous family members as to how close a connection she had with the milkman! In total contrast to my dark ethnic features, Bernice had fair skin, auburn hair and a pretty little nose. Henry clearly loved his daughter and treated her like a princess, but she did not resemble a Jewish one!

In her mid-teens, she flourished physically, transforming from a bespectacled girl in glasses into a swinging sixties chick. The attention of a number of local lads was aroused, causing the irrepressible Uncle Joe to comment that it was not just their attentions that grew. My mother's expectations leapt to previously un-dreamed-of heights when Bernice attracted the notice of an unexpected suitor at the Brady Club. The venerable Kemble family manufactured pianos and resided in the leafy suburbs of north-west London. Great benefactors of the less fortunate among the brethren, they demonstrated their support in money and action. The father and mother seemed almost like royalty when they graced proceedings. When my mother discovered that the son and heir was showing more than an academic interest in her second child, her romantic heart started to race. Sadly for her, Nancy's organ wasn't given the chance to sustain its frantic momentum. Bernice liked her admirer, but not sufficiently to even breathe the word *chupah*, the canopy placed over the bride and groom in a synagogue while the wedding service is conducted. When she informed my mother that she was going to end the barely-started liaison, my mother pronounced her *mershugger* (mad). You might have the instrument, but if you can't play the right tune.

Other marginally less favoured boyfriends followed. My mother's hopes rose again, though not to the previously Olympian heights, when a young Jewish dentist came to our door. He likewise was to suffer rejection. 'What more do you want?' cried my mother in disbelief. 'He's got his own practice in Pinner!' Despite this impassioned plea, Bernice refused to be pinned down.

Bernice then decided to visit Israel. Marriage to a Sabra would guarantee her a religious blessing, but could mean for my mother a separation of almost 2,000 miles from her only daughter and (please God) any future grandchildren. The thought of the yet-to-be-conceived children growing up in a war zone represented a fear in the back of her mind, but her worries were to prove groundless. My sister turned her back on the Promised Land after fruit picking on a *kibbutz* caused unacceptable damage to her finger nails!

During Bernice's Exodus, my father joined her for a few weeks courtesy of a rare good run at the races and El Al. His experiences in the Holy Land, and the feelings they gave rise to, probably differed from that of the average tourist. The many famous historic and religious places of interest appeared to have made little impact. What he marvelled at was the sight of Jewish policemen and . . . dustmen.

Inevitably, in the case of my unworldly father, the most embarrassing incident had a sexual connotation. One day, the pair checked in at a hotel in Tel Aviv. Bernice noticed that, when my father asked at reception for a room with two single beds (as a cost-saving exercise), the clerk gave them a knowing smile when handing them the key. On entering the restaurant for the evening meal, they felt that many critical eyes were slyly and strangely turned on them. This was followed by the feeling that many of the comments passed between the occupants of the other tables concerned themselves. They ignored as best they could the somewhat disturbing atmosphere and tried to enjoy their kosher meal. As my father was about to take a sip of red wine, an interrupting cough prevented the glass from reaching his lips. He looked up into the disapproving face of an elderly woman standing above him. She clearly did not approve, for some reason, of the smart middle-aged man and the beautiful girl. 'Anything wrong?' asked my innocent and bemused father. 'Yes, you,' replied the lady in a thick mid-European accent. 'You disgust me. She is young enough to be your daughter!'

## seventeen

# Morris Minor

Following my grandmother's death, her flat was occupied by my mother's youngest brother Morris, his wife Rene and baby son Larry. Morris was the spitting image of David Suchet's *Inspector Poirot*. He had a gentle sense of humour and, like me, he took a particular delight in puns! My sympathy for him was particularly aroused when my mother informed me that, in the times of hardship after the First World War, my grandmother would attempt to assuage his hunger with cheese rind. Years later, my most vivid manner memory of him is of hot late summer afternoons when his chosen manner of relaxing after work was to place a deck chair outside 5 Herbert House beside the infamous dust chute. Firmly ensconced in his canvas seat, with a much-mocked knotted handkerchief protecting his bald head, he would happily read the *London Evening News* surrounded by thousands of particles of dust.

Before dying of an unexpected heart attack, Morris developed a less life-threatening condition when a problem was diagnosed in the upper thigh, his walking was impaired, and he was required to use a supporting stick to get about. Observing Morris and his restricted movement, a concerned friend asked him how he was feeling. Morris replied, 'The hip's not too good but the stick's getting better.'

My cousin Larry was accorded the unfathomable nickname of 'Bowser'. He inherited his father's love of comedy and cricket – Uncle Morris was one of the few Jews to cross the Thames and enter the Oval. Larry and I preferred the other great ground on the north-west frontier – Lord's. With sandwiches and flask packed in a duffel bag, he and I spent much of the school summer holidays in our early teens on the upper tier at the Nursery End. From its back row, we would observe proceedings on the hallowed turf in front of us and, by turning our heads, could watch the hopeful young professionals in the nets of the practice ground. We were the proud possessors of score books in which we recorded the match statistics in painstaking detail.

From this lofty perch, I began to smoke a pipe. When not present at cricket's headquarters, I often listened to the radio commentary where the soft beguiling tone of John Arlott's Hampshire burr became music to my ears. When his face appeared on giant-sized advertising hoardings or in TV commercials, expressing delight at smoking St Bruno tobacco, I was converted. By a process of trial and error, once my own equipment had been purchased, I worked out the correct amount and density of flake to be inserted in the bowl of the pipe. When I had mastered the technique of puffing unhurriedly and contentedly without the constant need to relight the contents, my satisfaction equalled the attainment of O-level certificates.

Larry played as well as spectated. He was a steady, workman-like batsman, who struggled with his running between the wickets. When partnering him, the thought of a quick single never entered your head.

## eighteen

# Barking Mad

The family were split geographically into two almost equally divided sections as a number of aunts had bettered themselves in the late 1940s and, with herd instinct, decided to move in a lemming-like dash to Barking.

Aunt Annie married Sidney Levy. Sid's part-time employment assembling and dismantling stalls with Uncle Aaron provided only a minute proportion of his income. His main source of revenue came from his weekly work in the printing trade, producing one of the big daily newspapers.

Their two children, Rosie and Larry, played bit parts in my life in contrast to the more permanent roles of those who lived closer at hand. Rosie is about ten years my senior. She was an attractive blonde bombshell – a Little Miss Dynamite. A naturally stagey person, her sudden bursts into song delighted us. Her *pièce de résistance* was what I thought of as the 'telephone number' – Rose Murphy's 'Busy Line'. It was one of those catchy numbers that families request the performer to reproduce time and time again.

In 1954, my parents decided on a rare August holiday in the Cavendish Hotel, Cliftonville, Kent. They hoped that, in addition to providing Bernice and me with daytime fun, they would have some time to themselves in the evenings. Not the sort to abandon their children, even for a few hours, they decided to offer Rosie the job of babysitter. Events did not go entirely to plan. One evening, my parents returned to find their offspring sitting on the top step of the hotel entrance pitifully awaiting their return. My flighty cousin had gone AWOL with Tom, Dick and possibly Harry. Fortunately no long-lasting damage was done. My own postscript was that Rosie Levy should henceforth be called 'Rosie Levum'. What she did in fact become was Rosie Lewis. Her husband Laurie succeeded in anchoring her after National Service in the Royal Navy.

Mum, Bernice, me and Dad on our 1954 Cliftonville holiday.

It was during that Cliftonville holiday that I was given a salutary and never-to-be-forgotten history lesson. On a day when the sun decided to shine and the temperature rose into the 70s, we headed for the clifftop lift to take us down to the beach, Bernice and I carrying the regulation buckets and spades. On arrival at sea level, my parents hired deck chairs and set up camp while we made a start on sandcastles to be adorned with pebbles and matchsticks. When I needed a break from the construction industry, I made my way into the water. My mother had warned me to keep to the shallows and not venture too far out. The warning was unnecessary as I was a poor swimmer. As soon as I could not feel the sand when my feet searched for it after thirty seconds of strained doggy paddle, I headed back to the nearby shore.

That morning, while idly and safely disturbing 6 inches of water, I found myself being watched by another boy. He seemed friendly. I told him my name and he replied that his was Julian but he pronounced it in an odd way. After playing together for a few minutes, two long shadows fell across us. We looked up, and Julian smiled and introduced his parents. Like him, they spoke with an accent but it was more pronounced. I somehow knew they were Jews but that they were different.

During the brief conversation, I noticed that both his parents, on their lower arms, had numbers etched into their flesh. They caught my stare and a brief pained expression crossed their faces. The moment passed. Leaving the water together, I pointed to where my parents were sitting. Nancy waved and Julian's parents raised their hands in polite acknowledgement. Nancy then proceeded to beckon us. Julian's mother and father looked questioningly at each other then nodded. It took about fifty footprints in the sand to reach my curious parents where mutual greetings took place. While Julian and I knelt to resume work on the castle with Bernice, our respective parents began to talk.

Looking up occasionally from our spadework I noticed that, although the foursome were clearly getting on, the conversation was muted. Henry kept looking down at the striped canvas between his legs, and Nancy surprisingly had tears in her eyes. All this seemed out of kilter on a lovely day at the English seaside. Back in our hotel room, I asked my mother about the mysterious numbers on the arms. She explained after a pause, 'There was a place called Auschwitz. . .'

Rosie's younger brother Larry was somewhat nearer in age to me. I would have liked to have seen more of him but Barking seemed a long way from the East End. He was responsible in part for perhaps my first betrayal when I allowed him to convert me from Spurs to Arsenal for a few years. He obviously believed he was doing it for the best of motives.

In his late teens he journeyed to the Brady Club and became a regular in the soccer team. As a towering centre-half, he relished going upfield into the opposition's penalty area for corners. He announced his arrival with the cried instruction to the kicker of 'far post'. When he became another of the cabbie cousins, his nickname on the ranks turned into 'Far Post Larry'.

My mother was as fond of him as of all her nephews but she became alarmed when the family was informed that he was getting serious about a non-Jewish girl. Annie was instructed by her sisters to admonish her son and warn him of the inherent dangers if he took matters further. He listened and obeyed. There was an ironic twist to his love life. He eventually married a native Israeli girl who according to Rosie (despite the blessing of two daughters) made his matrimonial life one of sheer misery. The marriage ended in divorce.

I met Miriam on only a couple of occasions but this was sufficient to appreciate what Larry had undertaken, and she seemed to personify the self-confidence, critics might say arrogance, of the Israelis. She had unshakable opinions on everything and could express and defend them in effective English.

This was her second but not her only other language. No family member could even think of challenging her in her native modern Hebrew. She was a tall, brown-eyed, black-haired muscular amazon. Whether Larry was the victim of domestic violence is not known. One assumed, however, that she carried quite a punch, as well as a powerful and accurate throwing arm.

Years after their separation, Rosie related a story about Miriam of almost Biblical quality, it would have impressed the warriors of the Old Testament. Miriam was driving along an isolated dusty road in her homeland when she spotted ahead of her what appeared to be an Israeli soldier, thumbing a lift. It is customary in Israel for private motorists to stop for any member of the nation's Defence Forces. Miriam dutifully picked up the 'soldier' who then occupied the front passenger seat at her side. She was about to pull away when suddenly the disguised Arab produced a knife and held it to her throat. In a flash, Miriam retaliated. She disarmed her would-be attacker with consummate ease and proceeded to beat and tie him up. This superwoman then conveyed her parcelled Palestinian to the nearest police station. There, the presumably astonished constabulary relieved her of her charge, and placed him in custody. That night, Miriam's exploit made national news.

Sadly, Larry later contracted cancer and became the first of my cousins to die. Miriam attended Larry's funeral, and the assembled mourners sadly witnessed her total and clearly genuine devastation. The countless tears proved that in her own particular way, she must have loved him.

## nineteen

# Monty Mania

My Aunt Lily was arguably the most glamorous of my mother's sisters on the evidence of early photographs. When she married the other Monty Levine, she also took up residence in Barking, although in a quieter area than the one lived in by the Levys.

Monty had spent most of the Second World War in the hotspots of the East, mainly in India and Burma. Despite this prolonged stay in a tough, masculine environment, he had a prissy streak. He once told me in quite a serious and disapproving tone that once, while on guard duty, a native girl offered him 'Jiggy Jiggy'. He could perhaps have added that this was the closest he came to seeing any action.

On his return to civilian life, he acquired a market stall and sold chickens in the lane on weekdays. Monty was affectionate and tactile and, if I inadvertently came close, would pinch my cheeks in greeting. This was clearly meant as a warm gesture but I did not relish the touch of fingers stained, like those of Mr Goldstein, my Hebrew teacher, with the blood of dismembered fowls. In contrast, when at home, Monty was so clean and tidy that he drove family visitors to distraction. In the summer, anyone re-entering his terraced house from the back garden (with its couple of prized plants) had to submit to a shoe inspection. Once inside, whenever he spied a bit of crisp, nut or an olive stone on his fitted carpets, he would leap from his chair. With brush and pan, or in later years a vacuum cleaner, he would remove the offending morsels without any consideration for the comfort or feelings of his guests. References to 'Mad Monty' were inevitable. Some suggested that prisoners should pay their debt to society by being compelled, for the duration of their sentence, to live with him. Lily, however, could say things others could only think. When his mania could not be tolerated for another moment,

Burmese days, Monty standing with belt.

she would simply tell him to 'f**k off'. The family considered her language restrained.

I was always aware of the need to treat Monty's fixtures and fittings with respect and to ensure, on entry and exit, that I heard the click of his garden gate. He warned me that carelessness could lead to the front path being plastered with 'dogs' do-do'.

Lily and Monty's only child was Frankie. He was my closest cousin in age and the second in the family to go to university. As boys we got on well and visits to his house were keenly anticipated. Monty was a generous father and Frankie had a superior collection of toys to mine. In summers, as we

A family gathering featuring my mother (centre) holding Lorraine, and Lily and Monty's Frankie (right) with Bernice in front.

grew older and were allowed to wander off on our own, we loved to visit Barking Park where there was an open-air pool and tennis courts. But we were always careful to remove our shoes and deal with our wet swimming gear on our return!

# twenty

# Roses

Across the road from the Levines lived Aunt Emily and Uncle Lou Rose, the only childless couple among my close relatives. Like Monty, Lou had seen war service. A surviving photograph reflects a confident Lou proudly displaying his sergeant's stripes won during the Normandy campaign. On his return to England he worked in the clothing industry. Aunt Emily was similarly employed in the *shmateh* trade, rising to the rank of manageress. She was the only career woman among her sisters. Her success in business enabled her to enjoy the high standard of living which, to her credit, she allowed the rest of the family to enjoy. The Roses spearheaded the family's entry into the new 'affluent society' of the late 1950s. Lou, in his smart cloth cap, relished washing and polishing his new Ford Zephyr in full view of his admiring or envious neighbours. In summer, a new noise was heard emanating from his back garden as Lou was also the first uncle to own a motorised lawn mower.

Emily's materialism matched that of her husband, and she was the first aunt to purchase (not hire) both a washing machine and a spin dryer. Her acquisition of household gadgets resulted in her kitchen reverberating to novel sounds – the whirr of a food processor and the ping of a pop-up toaster while cups of tea were dispensed speedily with the aid of a gleaming electric kettle. Pride of place in the lounge was given to a 21-inch Ferguson television. Uncle Morris dubbed this flagship item the 'Massive-Ferguson'.

On hot summer days, while Emily reclined on her padded lounger, smearing herself with Ambre Solaire, the background music was provided by a portable radio. However, the electrical item that really held the family spellbound was a Grundig tape recorder. One of the greatest shocks of my early life was to hear my own voice coming out of that machine.

The Roses attended a number of prestigious functions that my mother, basking in the reflected glory, boasted about to listeners in the lane. Lou and Emily impressively obtained tickets to a Royal Command Performance at the London Palladium and to the first night of *My Fair Lady*, starring Rex Harrison, Julie Andrews and Stanley Holloway at the Theatre Royal, Drury Lane.

Emily was the 'hostess with the mostest'. Her generosity matched that of Joe and, on Christmas Day, it was at her house that the biggest and best party was thrown. Although it was only a semi, it seemed a palatial residence to us and could accommodate most of the family. There was more than enough to eat and drink with Aunt Emily constantly urging us to refill our plates. We loyally watched the Queen's television broadcast, for Emily was a fervent royalist. Dickie Overs wisely kept his thoughts on the subject to himself during the programme as he didn't want to jeopardise the offer of free nosh.

At some stage in the evening, someone would burst into song and the sisters would go through their repertoire, starting with their rendition of Rosemary Clooney and Vera Ellen's 'Sisters' from the appropriately named *White Christmas*. During this song they rose *en masse*, held arms and danced around the room to the huge embarrassment of their husbands and children. We would then entertain ourselves with traditional cockney favourites like 'Knees up Mother Brown', 'My old Man said follow the Van', 'Down at the Old Bull and Bush' and 'I'm shy Mary Ellen, I'm shy'. Uncle Joe's party-piece was a comic number entitled 'One Night in Gay Paree' referring in part to an unwelcome mother-in-law. As a boy, I rightly suspected it had a hidden salacious meaning which went above my head. I did, however, laugh at the lines 'Last night I greased the stairs, put tin tacks on the chairs.'

When they could take no more of the 'entertainment', the men would withdraw to the kitchen and Emily's formica-topped table for a few hours of Solo – the working man's Bridge. I was allowed to watch, but not speak, and was fascinated by the various moves. I willed Lady Luck to favour my father as a great many silver coins, and sometimes even a note, would move around the table. After every game, there would be a burst of recriminations between partners as to why certain tricks were lost.

Back in Emily's living room, the aunts would reminisce about old times or talk about who had been recently taken ill or died, or run off with someone else's husband. This would take place against the sound of brazil nuts or walnuts being cracked open. Few relatives could be accommodated overnight and a high price was paid for a hired car to ferry us back to the East End at the end of the evening.

When I was in the sixth form at school, I became indebted to Emily and Lou for a particularly gracious favour. Once determined on an attempt to enter

Uncle Lou and Aunt Emily – the Roses.

university, I required a much quieter atmosphere in which to study than the one provided by 4 Barnett's Mansions. When my predicament became known to Emily, she offered me free bed and board until the summer A-level exams of 1963. In the event I lived with the Roses from Monday to Friday, and in that childless home I found the necessary tranquillity to bury myself in my books.

Each day, I would take the District Line from and to Upney station with the fare being paid by my parents, supplemented by pocket money from the generous Emily and Lou.

The relationship worked both ways. My aunt seemed for a while to regard me as the son she never had, and when she referred to me as 'Junior' I felt the Americanism was tinged with sadness as well as humour. I appreciated what my parents and aunt and uncle were doing for me and there was never any need for anyone to tell me to work. In fact, they often said 'Jeffrey, why don't you go out tonight?' On reflection, they may have occasionally wanted me out of the way.

D-Day invader,
Uncle Lou Rose.

It was a monkish existence, a largely sterile period during which I'd often sit biting the end of my biro thinking in a bitter-sweet way of my ex-girlfriend Janice Bowman and her quirky physical charms. She spoke with a studied lisp, believing this to be sexy, which it was. I found her face attractive despite (or perhaps because of) its slightly broken nose. The origin of this feature intrigued me but I never summoned the courage to ask how she came by it. The body, just above average height, curved in all the right places. Foolishly, I two-timed her with a hairdresser. Lucille worked in a salon within walking distance of the school and one lunchtime, unbeknown to me, I was spotted canoodling with her by a friend of Janice. During a literature lesson that afternoon, one of Janice's shoes was hurled across the classroom, hitting the side of my unfaithful head, causing it to bleed slightly. The set text was the *Merchant of Venice*, and Janice had had her pound of flesh.

The size 5 was not my final punishment. During her last year, a handsome young English teacher rode into the school car park on his Lambretta. I feared his none-too-discreet flirting with Janice might be successful. Her leaving the school in July was the green light and his motorised division legally moved in – I had been well and truly 'petrol pumped'. Standing lonely and forlorn at the bus stop or on a station platform, I grieved for some time for my raven-haired virago. That year the study of *The Taming of the Shrew* might have been a more appropriate Shakespearean play!

The broken heart was partly mended in the Lower Sixth when I dated Pauline Simmons. She was tall with a fair complexion. Despite her height, she went around the school with the year's shortest inhabitant and it was this which may have initially aroused my attention. She certainly had a most caring way with her vertically challenged friend. The fact that she had the sweetest of natures made me wish later that I had behaved more honourably towards her and her father. A glib-tongued classmate worked part-time in a local haberdasher's shop. One day he persuaded me to purchase, at below wholesale price, a batch of shirts which I believed I could easily sell on at a profit. Pauline's dad was my first and, as it turned out, only customer. To his surprise and annoyance and my discomfiture, when he tried on one of the shirts, it only reached his belly button and I had to return his money. It was a bad business move; I had been 'shirt-changed'.

The relationship with his daughter initially managed to survive the aborted transaction and, for a while longer, I enjoyed escorting Pauline. After our dates, the promenade home to her Ocean Estate flat on the Mile End Road took us past the infamous Blind Beggar public house. Just a few years after Pauline and I strolled innocently hand in hand past its doors, within them a gangland shooting was carried out by one of the Kray brothers. Had I known of the possibility of such goings-on at the time, it might well have curtailed my ardour at the foot of Pauline's stairwell.

1962/3 was my most important academic year but it was full of events of far greater significance in the wider world. The end of 1962 was marked by a most dramatic development in the weather as, on 27 December, the snow arrived unrequested from the North Pole. The temperature went down and stayed down until March. Trudging every day through the snow to and from the station from my lodgings fed my historical fancy. When particularly tired and weighed down by a baggage of bulky books, I imagined myself part of the 1812 Retreat from Moscow. Fortunately, in Upney Lane there were no spear-carrying Cossacks.

In June 1963, the Profumo scandal had raised the nation's libido and its temperature. In my semi-enforced celibacy, I was transfixed by the image of Christine Keeler sitting astride that incredibly lucky chair. Mandy Rice-Davies ('He would say that, wouldn't he?'), in tight skirt and high heels, tripping along the London pavements, was another powerful sexual image. I readily understood why the Minister for War had been eager to use his main armament. Like many of my contemporaries, I relished the teasing of the establishment on the new TV satirical programme, *That Was the Week that Was*. How appropriate that, in the coldest of years, its front man should have been David Frost. Aunt Em's conservatism and puritanism didn't find anything funny in the programme's university-style humour.

I had felt the same way about the Cuban Missile Crisis as I was convinced that neither Kennedy nor Khrushchev would back down, and that nuclear annihilation was imminent. In October 1962, I went through daily life like a zombie, believing my own petty ambitions pointless. For the first and only time, I experienced depression. The night I climbed Aunt Em's stairs, having just heard on the news that in the coming small hours the Russian missile-carrying merchantmen would be sunk by the US fleet, I believed them to be the stairway to heaven, my bedroom the departure lounge to eternity. Unbelievably waking the next morning, I dashed into the kitchen to hear on the portable radio that the world had come back from the brink. Never had the smell of fresh toast been so good. My life and appetite were back. The previously condemned man ate a hearty breakfast.

There was an unusual sequel to my tortured mental state on what I was convinced would be the last day of the world. I had decided that there was no earthly point in doing the A-level French translation exercise that Jimmy Lloyd had set for that evening. When I was required to face him the next morning with the assigned work not even attempted, let alone completed, I had to provide an explanation. On hearing my reasoning, he countered with a very stern expression on his face that there could be no excuse where his all-important subject was concerned. He then added, with a Gallic twinkle in his eye, 'And that includes World War Three!'

## twenty-one

# Swan Song

Kitty was the last of the aunts to move to Barking, helped by a deposit on the house supplied by Uncle Joe. This aunt had married Alf Swan who had been Swandanovitch in an earlier elongated form. In the late 1940s and '50s, they had occupied a pokier flat than ours in a tenement block beside Toynbee Hall. Lovable Kitty was the dippiest of my aunts and her choicest utterances were regularly quoted for the benefit of fresh ears. Many years later when Cousin Frank had made his million and was playing host to Kitty, a far wealthier man arrived at the country house by helicopter. After listening to his catalogue of travels around the world, Kitty earnestly enquired if he had ever been to Benidorm. Before the slightly stunned but well-bred gentleman could reply, she added that she recommended it.

Kitty was a mistress of malapropisms. Once, on entering Rosie's house and noticing the mist on the inside of the windows, she had no hesitation in passing comment. She informed my astonished cousin that 'the compensation was terrible!' On another occasion, Rosie and Kitty were discussing their favourite TV programmes. Kitty enthusiastically recommended a new American programme called *Lalaw*. Rosie was completely mystified and asked Kitty to repeat the title. This she did by simply raising her voice – 'LALAW'. Understanding still eluded my confused cousin but Rosie became aware of her husband Laurie chuckling in the background. He gave his wife a wink, unseen by her aunt, and asked Kitty if she could possibly go into the kitchen and make them all a nice cup of tea. This she obligingly did and, in her contrived absence, Laurie picked up their daily newspaper's TV guide and pointed without a word to Kitty's new 'must-see' programme. Rosie read the title herself – *L.A. Law*.

I owed much to Kitty as, in infancy, she had looked after me during a number of Nancy's medical crises. Her most-needed nursing occurred when my mother miscarried with twins who would have been two years my junior had they survived. Perhaps the fickle balance of nature was redressed when my own twin boys came into the world almost forty years later.

Alf was a distinctive figure due to his shock of wiry red hair. He had a soft spot for his nephew and took me on a number of outings. A trip to London Zoo in Regent's Park was the most dramatic. A pleasant but unremarkable day was immortalised as we passed through the dromedary paddock. While Alf was preoccupied with holding my hand to ensure that I came to no harm, one of the camels took a liking to the colour and texture of his hair and proceeded to help himself to a chewy mouthful. Alf naturally got the 'hump'. The zoo officials were apologetic but these were not litigious times and, as far as I know, my scalped uncle received no compensation. Instead, Alf had the indignity of travelling home with a ridiculous area of white skin amid his flame-coloured hair which was standing on end with the shock of being headhunted.

Kitty and Alf's daughter Lorraine was close to Bernice in age and provided her with companionship at family gatherings. She was a bubbly child whose giggle amused rather than irritated. The only black mark against her was her choice of youth club. In her teens, when able to travel from Barking, she declined to join Brady. Instead she took herself to the Oxford and St George's Club which, in spite of its name, was also a predominantly Jewish one. In fairness to Lorraine who saw herself as a singer and tap dancer, Oxford offered more in the way of acting opportunities. It put on a number of musicals including, in the early 1960s, *The Boy Friend* starring the subsequently famous Henry Goodman whose sister Rita was Lorraine's best friend.

Once settled in Barking, Alf and Kitty became the poor relations among those living there. But we could never have foreseen how brief my uncle's residence in suburbia was to be. Suddenly and sadly, disaster struck in 1964 when Alf, only in his forties, suffered a fatal heart attack. It was the first such tragedy to shock us all. Kitty, highly emotional in normal circumstances, was distraught and Lorraine was shell-shocked.

Surprisingly, my aunt's lonely widowed state did not last long. One of Alf's workmates, Geoff Nobbs, followed up the paying of respect with a whirlwind and effective courtship of the recently bereaved wife. Disapproving words were uttered about Kitty's non-Jewish friend but she was completely smitten and would not be deflected from the course of true and new love. They were married with what many regarded as unseemly haste although Lorraine appeared happy with her new stepfather. Geoff proved to be a devoted husband and gave my aunt a few years of happiness before he in turn passed away. Kitty had the unwished-for distinction of being the only sister to be widowed twice.

To me, Geoff was a bit of a hero. As a sailor during the war, he had served on the dreaded convoys to Russia, claiming this had turned his hair prematurely white. I listened attentively to his stories of life in the Senior Service. I handled with care, and studied with interest, his collection of black and white and sepia photographs that were its pictorial record.

Geoff presented a pleasantly contrasting figure at family functions as he always sat with a true Englishman's pint in his hand. He gradually picked up the odd word or phrase of Yiddish. On returning from the honeymoon he declared that he had never been so snug in bed – his lean frame was now gloriously heated by Kitty's *tookas* (bum).

To balance the historical record, I should add that not everyone found Kitty so amusing and endearing. Lorraine's husband Alan certainly fell into this category as it was clear how much strain Kitty put on his nerves. Alan was one of those rare Jewish boys who decided to join the peacetime British Army and served in Northern Ireland. He was a heavy-set bull of a man, a natural for yomping with a 60lb pack attached to his broad back and shoulders. The adrenalin rush brought on by a physical challenge or threat appealed to his psyche. The thought of firing a rifle with live ammunition added an extra buzz.

On leaving the Army with an impressive service record, he would not settle for a desk job and joined the London Fire Brigade. He was to enjoy being in the hotspots and candidly admitted that he and his colleagues, after hours of inactivity, relished a 'show', the latter being the term for a fire or some other challenging emergency. While he seemed a man without fear, he became edgy or irritable when in the presence of his mother-in-law. The nerves that neither bomb, bullet, nor conflagration seemed to trouble, twitched alarmingly when Kitty was close by. Lorraine's role as peacemaker must have been a tough one and the uneasy triangle possibly contributed to the collapse of the marriage.

Towards the end of her life, Kitty was housed in a granny flat built on to the side of the couple's larger house in Romford. One had the impression that Alan would have preferred her house to have been of the detached variety – at a distance of some miles.

## twenty-two

# Distant Dinah

Only one aunt lived on the west side of London – Dinah, who married Jack Watkins (Watchinski). Although not in Emily's league financially, having lived for many years in shared rented accommodation, Dinah gave herself airs and affected a middle-class accent. As a young woman, she was apparently the family's smartest dresser. Whatever job she had, the bulk of her pay was spent on clothes and cosmetics. Her poise only slipped a bit when one of the sisters 'borrowed' an item of clothing without permission.

On one occasion, however, it was Dinah who did the borrowing, and Ray didn't mince words in referring to this betrayal of family trust. The property in question belonged to the young Joe who sold a huge number of newspapers every day on a busy street corner. Each evening, on his return to the family's overcrowded accommodation, he would drape his jacket with its coin-filled pockets over the back of a chair. He soon began to suspect that unknown hands were stealthily helping themselves to the treasure trove. Sensing that Dinah did not want to meet his eye, she became the prime suspect. Joe's detective work inevitably meant that his entrapment of the culprit would involve his wicked sense of humour. He was aware that his erring sister had a horror of little furry creatures, so he placed two pieces of artificial scarlet fluff inside his bulging pockets. That evening, the air of the apartment was rent by a piercing scream and 'Dinah the Dip' was caught red-handed.

Despite this shaming experience, Dinah maintained an air of refinement, wearing prim little hats and neat leather gloves. She was the only sister who never allowed a swear word to soil her faintly lipsticked lips.

Jack was a little man with swarthy skin, causing me to wonder whether he was jaundiced. Of all the uncles, he professed to be the most religious – his Yiddish vocabulary was certainly the most extensive. It puzzled me that Dinah, who tried to present the image of a genteel English lady, should have attached herself to a man so clearly and proudly 'of the Faith'.

Their daughter Clare falls into the category of a long-lost cousin who, as with Dennis's elder brother Louis, I only saw on one occasion. The main reason for this is that she emigrated to Canada in the mid-1950s, a major blow to her parents but perhaps they were the cause of her defection? The family learned later of her engagement and marriage abroad and, more sensationally and ironically in view of the nature of her father's devotions, of a Catholic wedding ceremony. She returned to these shores from time to time to visit selected members of the family. Perhaps surprisingly, Clare's strongest bond was with Kitty who was one of the few to visit her in her adopted country.

## twenty-three

# Rich Kid

In addition to the official ones, my mother's friendships brought one or two courtesy aunts into my life, Bella Rich being the most noteworthy. In the early 1950s, she and her family accepted an invitation from the LCC to leave the East End and move to a new housing estate way out west. A glance at the map indicated that Harrow was on the far reaches of the Metropolitan Line. My mother was one of the first to receive an invitation to stay with her and I was excited to learn that we were destined to venture even further afield than Barking.

On arrival, we discovered a house with three bedrooms, inside and outside toilets and a back garden. Most significant of all, however, was the fact that no other family had ever lived in it. For the first time in my life, it dawned on me that, despite the knowledge that I enjoyed a happy childhood, it was nevertheless a deprived, inner-city one. When I stepped out of the house the next morning into bright sunlight and fresh air, this feeling was reinforced. The grass glistened and the flowers sparkled with dew drops. Hedges contained spiders' webs of incredible complexity and delicacy. Birds sang and the wind had a freshness it lacked when it whistled down city streets.

Stephen was the 'rich kid' who became my guide and mentor as I was led to the fields and woods which were only a stone's throw from their new abode. I discovered trees were there to be climbed and ponds to paddle in. Squirrels and rabbits could be observed in their natural habitat, and Stephen showed me birds' nests full of marvellously coloured eggs.

Stephen and his playmates all possessed bicycles with three-speed gears. I was invited to try them and to experience the adrenalin rush of free-wheeling down hills without recourse to the pedals. Most of the children also had pets and I witnessed for the first time the delight the animals gave their owners.

Rich kids – my mother sits left with Bernice in front, Bobby Rich sits in the centre and on the right Stephen Rich sits in front of Bella.

Dogs were not encouraged in our tenement blocks where there was often not enough room for the people, let alone animals. There were other surprises. For example, one boy was presented with an air rifle for his birthday while I was there and one girl went horse riding. I thought only Roy Rogers did that on the TV with his faithful horse Trigger.

Another novelty was the daily arrival of the ice cream van heralded by its loud jaunty signature tune. Kids would descend on it like a swarm of excited bees in an attempt to be first in the queue. We were then presented with an agonising choice from the wide range of ices and lollies on offer.

One summer's day Stephen led the way to Pinner Fair, involving a round trip of about 10 miles. This long walk came as an unwelcome shock to a boy used to hopping on and off London buses. An equivalent journey back home would have meant crossing three or four boroughs. I realised how puffed Dick Whittington must have felt at the top of Highgate Hill!

The elder brother Bobby commuted to London as a working man, and also sallied back and forth for pleasure on Saturday nights. I can recall first hearing from his lips of both Humphrey Lyttelton and his great jazz band and Lonnie Donegan and his skiffle group – whatever that was!

One of our returns to the City was particularly pleasurable for a train-spotter like me. We departed from Harrow and Wealdstone British Rail station, not the usual Overground-Underground route and our carriage was pulled by a steam train into London's Broad Street station. My excitement that day was, however, tempered by the knowledge that only a few years before Harrow and Wealdstone had made the front pages of all the newspapers and the BBC News for the wrong reason. In 1952, it was the scene of one of the worst rail crashes in the nation's transport history, involving an express train packed with passengers. The number of fatalities was so high that people were reminded of the number of civilians killed in many a wartime air raid.

Happily no such catastrophe occurred at Harrow-on-the-Hill. That station was for me, however, to be the scene of a repeated disappointment. Being a devotee of the Billy Bunter adaptations on TV and of Lord Snooty's weekly appearance in my comic, I was intrigued by the totally different world of the public schoolboy. I hoped therefore to actually spot one – a Harrow scholar in full rig. What did it feel like to have a straw boater on one's head? Sadly I never saw nor heard one on the platforms, ordering porters to carry their expensive gear. I assumed rightly that the real rich kids didn't travel on public transport!

## twenty-four

# Buster

My father's family seemed far less interesting than my mother's, but it did produce one colourful character. Henry's eldest sister Bessie had married Lou (widely known as Buster) Cohen (later Collins). He resembled the comedian Arthur English both in physical appearance and in his spivvy persona. Like the wide-boy Cockney comic, he was tall and thin and sported a toothbrush moustache. He wore loud suits, kipper ties and tilted trilby hats and as with that other great con-man, Private Walker of *Dad's Army* fame, he could get you anything if you were willing to pay the price.

By the early 1950s, Buster was into the 'Run Out'. This questionable business was, I assume, only marginally on the right side of the law. Those engaged in the enterprise would rent a market stall or empty shop on a short-term basis. Household goods would be acquired at bargain basement prices or lower. These would then be auctioned to a gullible public by a glib-tongued vendor. Buster was one of the best with gob and gavel. Two of his favourite maxims were 'a fool and his money are soon parted' and 'there's a mug born every minute'. He claimed to have sold Tower Bridge – three times. Buster could entrance an audience with his *spiel*. He could deal with hecklers with pearls of sarcasm and flatter old ladies with his charm. Given the privilege of an education, he might have stood for parliament.

In the mid-1950s, Buster's business provided me with the second best summer holiday of my childhood when I accompanied his team for a while on an away fixture in the Dorset seaside resort of Swanage. There they acquired a gaff on the seafront. It was a prime spot for crowd-pulling, standing as it did amid an array of amusement arcades, ice cream parlours and fish and chip shops. Buster's job was to pull the punters for the entire season and convince them that their lives would be devoid of value if they failed to buy his merchandise.

At the end of August the intention was to return to the less salty air of the big city with, as he put it 'a fat wedge in my kick'. This would line his pocket to withstand any adverse financial currents during a long winter.

In fairness, Buster was a devoted husband and father and he was determined to ensure that Bessie and my cousins David and Jessie enjoyed an all-expenses paid vacation courtesy of the yokels and the yobs. A large Victorian semi was rented and Aunt Bessie, presumably with Buster's approval, invited my mother, my sister and me down for a week. My father's commitment to the dogs and horses did not enable him to accompany us. This separation resulted in my first ever letter to him and, on my return home, I was pleased to find that he seemed to treasure it, and that the envelope bore such an exotic postmark. In the letter, I described the thrill of the railway journey from Waterloo, including the fascinating passage alongside Southampton Docks. As we trundled across a maze of points, I gazed up at the berthed trans-Atlantic liners which towered above us like huge iron cliffs, seemingly as tall as any building in the City of London. Their names were boldly printed in enormous lettering on their bows, equalling in interest those on my beloved steam locomotives.

Once there, the Swanage sand provided the raw material for the construction of sandcastles and for other games. I had my first horse ride on the beach, although the thrill was diminished somewhat by the handler simply walking the animal slowly up and down on a leading rein. I had had visions of riding cowboy-style over the breakwaters and galloping towards the horizon. In the water, there were other firsts. I sampled the delight of propelling a pedalo and floating in a rubber dinghy in the shallows.

My cousin David, who was to become, in material terms, one of my most successful cousins, was a weedy kid. One's skill at football determined your 'street cred'. In this respect, when captains tossed for team members, Davy had the indignity of being the last one picked. If the numbers involved were odd, a further blow was added to his self-esteem, when he became an option along with choice of goal or the right to kick off. I could have been more considerate, but I have to shamefully confess that I joined in the mickey-taking along with those who weren't related to him. Buster was fiercely supportive and, if he chanced to overhear or be informed of the ridicule dished out to his son, he would counter with a few choice words that had the effect of taking us down a justifiable peg or two.

I received a form of payback from David many years later. My wife and I were invited to the weddings of both his daughter and that of a stepdaughter. The arrival of the gilt-edged card constituted quite a surprise as we had not been on particularly close terms over the years. The ceremonies were held in the splendour of a West End synagogue with the proceedings accompanied by

Ride him Collins!

a string quartet. The banquets that followed were held in Park Lane hotels, the Dorchester and the Grosvenor House Hotel. They were both magnificent affairs. I wondered how close they came to rivalling the debutantes' balls of earlier decades. On studying the table plan at the first event, I realised my position in the social pecking order. Susan and I could not have been further away from the spotlight. Our chairs were between the potted palms and the service entrance at the rear of the hall. My wife had no need of the fan she had thought it advisable to bring, the gently waving fronds and the perpetually moving doors provided us with an effective draught.

Susan suffered a different kind of discomfort during that dinner, and I was regrettably the cause of her unease. I had always found the customary prayer session a monumental bore. When I saw the rabbi about to get to his feet, I asked Susan if I could be excused. In her innocence, this being her first Jewish wedding, she readily agreed. On my return half an hour later, I received a totally justified look of contempt. I didn't even pretend that I had been locked in the lavatory. In fact, I had spent the time in the book-lined reading room. Sitting in a beautiful armchair, I had idly leafed through one of the leather-bound volumes, taking gentle puffs on a Cuban cigar. Forgiveness was only shown some time later when Susan suggested we take to the dance floor for the 'slow one'!

When we hit the teenage years, Buster was forthcoming and explicit about sexual strategies. He relished witnessing our discomfiture when ignorance of word or deed was revealed, or when a failed exploit was reported to him. I nearly died when David informed him of a date I had with sexy Janice Bowman. As I left his flat, he leaned out of his window and yelled across the tenement yard 'Don't come in your pants!'

Buster's family owned a bakery and restaurant in Wentworth Street. Its delicious offerings often delayed us on the way home from school and if David was with us there was a real possibility of freebies. The personnel of the shop provided as much interest as the food in its window. David's Aunt Doris was the object of many speculative and not very charitable comments from some of my aunts. She looked like a tart and, while I doubt if she was active professionally, she certainly had an impressive array of boyfriends. On one return journey from the Saturday morning pictures with David, we entered the living quarters and Doris hailed us from behind her bedroom door. We entered the room and discovered her sitting up in bed unashamedly *décolletée*. Beside her, drawing on a Chesterfield, was a black man, while around a nearby chair was draped a uniform jacket of the American army. Doris was incredibly generous and, on this occasion, our pocket money was supplemented by her bedfellow. Her half-crown was joined by three packets of chewing gum. Doris's work in cementing Anglo-American relations received our total approval.

Buster's brother was the restaurant's proprietor, a smooth operator with a chic wife who looked more Cannes than Canning Town. Even in the dim recesses of the restaurant, she would sit disdainfully at a table in her shades, elegantly holding an elongated cigarette holder in manicured fingers. Their daughter Rosalind terrified me. At the age of fourteen, she must have been almost 6ft tall. She had a deep voice and a predatory manner.

Buster's friends provided as much colour as his family. Like Doris, Mad Jean would not have seemed out of place propositioning under the light of a lamp on a street corner; never did I see a woman in more make-up. The only individual to go close was the entertainer Danny La Rue who reproduced a similar rasp from his throat. The perfumes that emanated from her corseted body could overpower passers-by. I was always grateful if she came across us in the street that it was David who received her demonstrative hugs and kisses, and it was his feet that were menaced by her 6-inch stiletto heels. When we reached a more knowing age, we speculated about the chain she wore around her ankle. At sixteen and seventeen, we wondered how much she would charge.

'Nigger' Smith was allegedly the fastest driver in the East End. He reputedly established a record of one hour on the London to Southend road before its modernisation. One wondered whether his ability to pull away at speed and cause cars to disappear like lightning around corners was always used for legal purposes. Ironically, despite his daring image he was self-effacing, in marked contrast to Buster's bluster. How he came by his nickname I never discovered, but the last time I saw him it provided another moment of excruciating embarrassment. My parents spent the last year of their lives in a Jewish residential home in Tottenham. During their stay, 'Nigger' kindly paid a visit. This occurred during the serving of lunch, in a canteen staffed predominantly by West Indians. As he was shown into the eating area, my mother cried out in salutation, 'Hello Nigger.' The stunned silence was noisily broken by the sound of several dropped plates.

# Epilogue

It was in that hospice that my mother died of lung cancer in October 1990. Father, who had suffered for over a decade from MS, was to follow her in February 1991. The death certificate stated the cause of his death to be pneumonia, but I strongly suspected a broken heart. Since then, no day goes by without the two of them, however fleetingly, entering my thoughts. They did so much for me. I wish I had done more for them. I expect all children say that.

# Acknowledgements

The author would like to thank Jim Hickman, Joanne Jones, Vic Baker and Susan Rozelaar for their help and encouragement.